The Invisible Presence

Sixteen poets of Spanish America
1925-1995

The Invisible Presence

Sixteen poets of Spanish America
1925-1995

Poems Selected by Ludwig Zeller

Translated with an Introduction by Beatriz Zeller

Mosaic Press
Oakville, ON. - Buffalo, N.Y.

Canadian Cataloguing in Publication Data

The invisible presence : sixteen poets of Spanish America,
    1925-1995

ISBN 0-88962-546-8

1. Spanish American poetry - 20th century - Translations into English.   I. Zeller,
Beatriz.

PQ7087.E5I58   1996   861   C95-933366-5

Published by MOSAIC PRESS, P.O. Box 1032, Oakville, Ontario, L6J 5E9, Canada.
Offices and warehouse at 1252 Speers Road, Units #1&2, Oakville, Ontario, L6L
5N9, Canada and Mosaic Press, 85 River Rock Drive, Suite 202, Buffalo, N.Y.,
14207, USA.

Mosaic Press acknowledges the assistance of the Canada Council, the Ontario Arts
Council, and the Dept. of Canadian Heritage, Government of Canada, for their
support of our publishing programme. The translator wishes to thank the Ontario
Arts Council for its generous support toward the translation of this anthology.

Cover Collage by Ludwig Zeller
Translations by Beatriz Zeller
Book design by Susan Parker
Printed and bound in Canada
ISBN 0-88962-546-8

In Canada:
MOSAIC PRESS, 1252 Speers Road, Units #1&2, Oakville, Ontario, L6L 5N9,
Canada. P.O. Box 1032, Oakville, Ontario, L6J 5E9
In the United States:
MOSAIC PRESS, 85 River Rock Drive, Suite 202, Buffalo, N.Y., 14207

TABLE OF CONTENTS

INTRODUCTION

Poetry can only be an abyssal dialogue between a person and the world, between one's inner reality and the information that our senses provide, poured into the spectacle that is palpable reality. The poem is the sign of that dialogue and poetry can only be understood as the expression of a vital experience, of the whirlwind that results from emotion and desire, and above all, from the profound energy that gives rise to a poem: the demon of permanent insatisfaction.

These words by Enrique Molina describe the spirit which has guided the poets gathered in this anthology – poetry as an inescapable calling, as the ultimate adventure, poetry as the sole means of attaining the unreachable, the absolute.

Few can deny that the great voices of literature written in Spanish in the Twentieth Century are born in the Americas. After centuries of speaking the language of the invaders, of reciting traditional meters and forms imported from Spain, Latin Americans were ready for something new. The first two decades of our century witnessed the emergence of several poets who freed Spanish poetry from its static and moribund cadences and brought to it deep, often hoarse sounds which had lain there dormant, yet had never been articulated and expressed with such force and efficacy.

Important inroads had been made thirty years earlier by Rubén Darío from Nicaragua, who was the first poet after the long decadence of Spanish literature to infuse new life into the language. He did so by assimilating in part the ideas and forms of the Parnassian poets of France into Spanish poetry. The influence of "Modernismo," the literary and aesthetic movement he initiated, opened the doors of modernity to Spanish literature both in the Americas and in Spain.

The subsequent discoveries made by the avant-garde movements in Europe in the early part of our century and their quick integration into Latin American poetic discourse allowed poets like Gabriela Mistral, Vicente Huidobro and the inimitable César Vallejo to give voice to a reality which had until then not been expressed. Liberated from the constraints of traditional forms by the introduction of new techniques,

the Spanish language became the instrument whereby this new genera-
tion of poets began to explore ancient regions still alive in the popular
psyche. The cadences of indigenous folklore and a fearlessness in
coming face to face with the marvelous infused the Spanish language
with new found vitality. The legacy of the work accomplished by the
poets in the first half of this century, a veritable earthquake, can still be
felt today in all literary genres throughout the Spanish-speaking world.

Latin American readers know and cherish the great luminaries of
that period who, besides the aforementioned poets, include Pablo Neruda,
Jorge Luis Borges, Octavio Paz, José Lezama Lima. These poets have
become part of the canon. English-speaking readers are familiar with
their work through sporadic and often uneven translations which have
been published over the last 25 years. Yet there are a host of poets who
merit equal attention, whose work continues to have influence on
contemporary poetry, often in editions long ago out of print which
circulate almost privately among eager readers and writers. One of the
many reasons why these poets remain largely marginalized by the
literary establishment is their uncompromising, anarchic attitude to-
ward life and its expression through poetry. Many of the Latin Ameri-
can writers who attained international recognition chose to align them-
selves with a political party. Generally, although not exclusively, it was
certain factions of the Left which benefited from the promotion of poets
like Pablo Neruda, or Ernesto Cardenal. Unfortunately, the enormous
success that such promotion brought numerous writers was often at the
expense of many of their equally talented and prolific contemporaries
who chose to remain independent of political parties and their dogmas.
It is difficult for North Americans to conceive that culture can be thus
divided for the sake of political expediency. This much is certain,
against all odds the poets gathered in these pages chose to follow their
inner demons, to jump into the tumultuous waters of the spirit. They
are the "terrible workers" Rimbaud talked about, those damned to
conquer the dark side of the moon.

How did this anthology come to be? How did this multifaceted
being grow eyes, limbs, a beating heart? It all began when as a teenager
I would listen to Ludwig Zeller, under whose parental care I grew up,
read to me poems and stories by the writers he carried with him like
treasures, a few books salvaged from the veritable shipwreck that was
my parents' chosen exile in Canada. In this dialogue which we have
sustained for twenty odd years, the words of a whole group of poets

came alive for me though Ludwig's unique understanding of their work and their place within contemporary Spanish American poetry. Memories of his personal meetings with many of them enlivened our conversations, making my learning about that whole cosmology of poetry a joyful and passionate experience. At some point Ludwig suggested I try my hand at translating a couple of short essays by Aldo Pellegrini and soon after, "To Mayo," a long poem by Enrique Gómez-Correa. Discussing specific literary problems which inevitably arise from any translation lent extra richness and immediacy to our dialogues about poetry. I believe it was at that juncture that our collaboration began. All along Ludwig insisted on how important it would be to bring to light the contribution made by so many poets long obscured in Latin America, and that there was a need to set the record straight, as it were, to bring some balance in people's understanding of contemporary Spanish American poetry. It was in this manner that he conceived of this anthology. Although we have consulted constantly on what poems would sound best in English translation, his selection is what makes this anthology such a unique statement about Spanish American poetry.

I began by translating the poetry of Enrique Gómez-Correa. The directness of his poetry, and the surprising manner in which he makes the paintings of René Magritte come to life, move on the page, is remarkable:

Once the blindfold is removed
We find ourselves in the same room we visited before
The sun holds surprises for us sometimes
And without knowing why we now discover
The ghosts that disturb our tongues
The mind's shape itself.

Next, I translated the work of other members of "Mandrágora," the Chilean Surrealist group, active between 1939 and 1945. Gómez-Correa and Braulio Arenas were its animators, but the group included Teófilo Cid and the precocious genius, Jorge Cáceres, who joined their ranks at the age of 16. The ease with which Cáceres absorbed the purest values of universal literature, and the fact of his untimely death at the age of 26, helped me to understand that true poetry was that which could speak and communicate something fresh and alive to one like me, translating it some 35 years after it was originally written. Much like the French Surrealists, "Mandrágora" was a collective which sought to change the world through the celebration of love, through the exploration of the unconscious as it manifests itself in dreams and in madness. The result of this adventure are poems like Arenas' "The Courtyard," "The Cat" and "To The Hallucinating Beauties," which like Gómez-Correa's "The Slothful Ones," is born from the latter's research at the mental asylum of Santiago de Chile in preparation for his doctoral dissertation, *Sociology of Madness*.

Many poets came into the Surrealist orbit of "Mandrágora." Gonzalo Rojas is singular among them in style because along with the influence of Surrealism, one can discern in the directness with which he approaches his subjects the influence of the Spanish classics of the Golden Age. Rojas is adept at giving material form to the intangible, as in the poem "I Get Up at Four O'Clock" where a cat walking on the sidewalk suddenly becomes Mary Magdalene:

> ...And who should I meet
> When I step into the street but Magdalene
> ...ancient and mad Hebrew woman, hair unbound
> disguised as the whitest of white cats,
> lost in the night, badly injured by love.

Ludwig Zeller can be said to be the heir of "Mandrágora." He has followed the basic ideas of Surrealism with fervor, exploring them beyond orthodoxy and convention. Anna Balakian, in situating Zeller within Surrealism, has stated: "As in Breton's work, Zeller's dominating force is love, and in reality as in principle it integrates his universe... But there the resemblance stops. Zeller's poetry has totally shed the decorative and courtly language against which Breton as a pioneering poet struggled... Zeller spells out beauty in terms of total aesthetic revision, and his eroticism is both graphic and imminent."[1] In his introduction to Zeller's *In the Country of the Antipodes*, A.F. Moritz, on the other hand, has stated that "Zeller's imagery is baroque in the strict stylistic sense of the term. The Baroque is a 'genre of art uniquely Spanish,' as Garcia Lorca notes, and Zeller's imagery is most successfully viewed not as surrealist, but as an outgrowth of Spanish and Latin American baroque, which was refreshed between 1870 and 1930 with the help of Symbolism and Surrealism."

Zeller's case illustrates the perfect meshing that has taken place between classical Baroque as developed by the poets of the Golden Age in Spain and modern Surrealism. The manner in which both these styles mix in all genres of Latin American literature is essential to the understanding of twentieth-century Spanish American poetry, but such an analysis is beyond the possibilities of this introduction.

There are three great poles in Spanish American Surrealism: Mexico, Chile and Argentina. Mandrágora of Chile was perhaps the most coherent of the three groups. The Argentine group under Aldo Pellegrini's leadership can be said to be the most open, least orthodox of the three, with a surprising number of visual artists among its members. Pellegrini's greatest contribution is undoubtedly his efforts at disseminating Surrealist ideas in Latin America through translations, essays and poetry: he was the first Spanish American poet to write Surrealist verse intentionally. A close collaborator of Pellegrini's is Enrique Molina, perhaps Spanish America's greatest living poet. His poetry is rich in sensuality and nostalgia for exotic lands which come alive with a lushness and beauty comparable to the best poems of Neruda's *Residence on Earth*. Unlike the Nobel prize winner, however, Enrique Molina is a poet to be admired for the veracity of his commitment to the poetic spirit. André Coyné has stated that "The poetry of Enrique Molina does not *wish to say* anything: it simply speaks. It does not deal with concepts, only with images. These he organizes behind the veil of a seemingly logical incoherence according to the laws of the strictest, most concrete of all coherences... reiterating voices of wonderment and jubilation."

Olga Orozco, also from Argentina, shows her innate ability at giving voice to the marvelous when she states that a poem is merely "an elusive reflection on a miserly mirror, barely the opaque cartography of a dazzling voyage, barely an approximation to a centre that is always shifting." Her poems speak about shrouds and what lies behind them, about empty houses revisited by the poet in her imagination, about empty boots that conjure the presence of their original wearer. And in the process of exploring the invisible, Orozco's poems speak about poetry itself, about its essence and its reason for being.

Dissonance, an attempt at juxtaposing images dissimilar in the extreme, these are the trademarks of César Moro's work. They reflect a chosen estrangement from his native Peru and from everything that society at the time represented. Moro lived long periods of his life in France and in Mexico and wrote half his work in French. Moro's most powerful poetry was written during his sojourn in Mexico. Erotic, unmasked, the poet reveals himself completely through texts unique for the naked honesty with which they explore the facets of homosexual love. Especially in "Love Letter," Moro makes love for the other and fear of surrendering completely to desire analogous with the cosmos:

> *I think of your body making sky and supreme mountains*
> *out of the bed*
> *I think of the only reality*
> *with its valleys and shadows*
> *moist marble and black water mirrors for all the stars*
> *in each of your eyes.*

Rosamel del Valle can be counted among the most extraordinary poets Spanish America has produced. The impact of reading and translating his poetry is comparable to the effect of a barely perceptible breeze shaking a tree down to its very roots. The irrational, the marvelous, these are the sources of the sumptuous imagery which del Valle elaborates through the use of interior monologues and seemingly set phrases. The result is a universe where the poet engages in dialogue with his ghosts, where the invisible world is made palpable with a naturalness that makes it irresistible. Del Valle brings a new vision of the world into being as exemplified by "The Apostles' Bar" where several voices sustain a conversation of the most magical kind:

> *"Just let me remember. A foggy city.*
> *Everyone went by with their hands raised*
> *And the sea came out to greet them." I know. My wound*
> *Had borne its fruit on the sand and the wind opened*
> *And passed into the night. "When that woman slept*
> *On the grass the waves were bells..."*

Because they were close friends, Rosamel del Valle is often compared to Humberto Díaz-Casanueva. Both were deemed "hermetic" by their contemporaries although their poetry is quite dissimilar in content and form. Díaz-Casanueva is more obviously a poet concerned with ideas. His education in philosophy in Jena, the admitted influence of Heidegger and Jaspers, of German Romanticism and Expressionism are fundamental to understanding Díaz-Casanueva's poetry. An ontological and existential search, a preoccupation with ethics and aesthetics expressed through analogies and symbolic imagery, is at work in Díaz-Casanueva as he attempts to disentagle the enigma of man's existence.

Eduardo Anguita's work is also considered "hermetic," but unlike that of his compatriot Díaz-Casanueva, his poetry does not concern itself with dialectical tensions. Rather, his verse would make one believe that he is enamored with a particular *mental* image. For example in "The Polyhedron and the Sea:"

> *"I was given a polyhedron as I stood by the sea,*
> *a solid yet invisible body...*
> *...How sweet to let myself slip along its edges*
> *faster than eyes turning toward the sun*
> *blind flight along a pristine line leading me to the*
> *encounter*

The poet oscillates between religious conviction and satanic malediction. Clearly there is a desire to explore the mechanisms of a world which we are condemned to never fully comprehend, to disentangle a purely mental or intellectual concept. The end result is poetry that shines with sheer convulsive beauty.

Automatism as a poetic technique has played an essential role in the development of twentieth-century Spanish American poetry. Pablo de Rokha is one of its best proponents. It is surprising to discover that after more than sixty years, his automatic text *South America* sounds as current, as fresh as if it had been written yesterday. De Rokha was certainly born before his time. Having lived in the shadow of two giants, namely Pablo Neruda and Vicente Huidobro, his poetry has until very recently not been published in its entirety, nor has it received the prestige it deserves. Of all the poets in this anthology de Rokha is the most *material*. The eroticism of his verse is born of de Rokha's perception of nature as a totality. His is a complete, unadorned vision of nature's creative energy and its destructive, tellurian force. It is an excessive, almost Rabelaisian vision of reality as in "Diamond Toy:"

> *Raimundo wishes the black egg of night would*
> *burst forever like a timeless sea built from one infin-*
> *ity to another like this deep bed which ties them*
> *together embracing them with its dark honey so sharp*
> *spreading velvets like full lengths of tongues found*
> *dead in the yellows of our beloved beaches*

The vastness of the land, natural landscapes which cannot be tamed, and which when tamed will revert to their wild form, this element defines much of Spanish American literature and explains the ease with which it has adopted the basic principles of Surrealism and its predecessor Romanticism, especially French and German Romanticism. But whereas Romanticism idealized nature, Surrealism proprosed seeing it in its full potentiality: reality in its complete form, the invisible and the magical included. Contact with nature thus opens the doors to the transformation of being. This is evident in the poetry of de Rokha, but it also manifests itself in the work of Alvaro Mutis whose style and sensibility is very different.

Mutis explains the impression nature made on him as a child: "...The hacienda was situated not far from the central cordillera in *Tierra Caliente*... There were two large rivers, tumultuous waters surrounded by all kinds of trees and perfumes... It was true paradise. All of this, the contact with nature, animals, life at its most beautiful, appear in my poems..." One can almost hear the deafening sound of torrential rain on the zinc roofs in Mutis' poem "Nocturne:"

> *The rain is beating down on the zinc roofs,*
> *its presence sings, it keeps me away from sleep*
> *it leaves me stranded among restless growing waters*
> *in this freshest of nights which drips*
> *between the vaulted coffee branches.*

José María Arguedas is best known as a fiction writer and for the invaluable contribution he made to Latin American culture by translating and disseminating contemporary Quechua literature. His readers are less familiar with his poetry, even though it has contributed to the remarkable renaissance Peruvian poetry is currently undergoing. Arguedas expresses the painful existence of today's Indian people, but he also expresses his love for their world. In the process he creates a new cosmology where the jet plane is as powerful a metaphor for the "all seeing," for God, as the hummingbird was in the past. He wrote the poems included in this anthology in Quechua and later wrote Spanish versions of them:

> *"...Yes they call it "Jet"*
> *All the golden scales in all the seas and all the rivers*
> *could never shine like the jet shines.*
> *The fearful knife-edge of sacred mountains shines so*
> *small down below: it has become a sorry icicle...*

César Dávila Andrade belongs to the same tradition as César Vallejo and José María Arguedas. His sensibility has its origins in native Indian traditions and this fact makes him both mysterious and marginal. It also makes him an heir to the tragic fate of the native people of Latin America. His poetry deals with this subject almost exclusively and is a powerful testimonial to the horror of the past and the sadness of the present. There is no solace in Dávila Andrade's vision of modern man as an exile in his own land.

Rendering the work of such varied powerful voices into English has been an exhilarating and often emotionally difficult experience. While translating Dávila Andrade's work for example, I often felt that I was sinking under the weight of his tragic vision. Rosamel del Valle on the other hand inspired me to see the world differently for months on end. For the one translating it is difficult to separate the author from the text. This is especially true of poetry where the author bares his or her self completely, where the stakes for the creator are so high. For this very reason, I have come to the conclusion that there are poems or parts of poems which are not possible to render in another language and do justice to the original. This is especially true of Spanish poetry and the English language. The trajectory of the two literatures diverges greatly at crucial points. English literature does not assume the Baroque with the same intensity that Spanish literature does. And Surrealism which has entered Spanish American literature so naturally is forever being dismissed as a kind of affectation by critics in the English-speaking world. Literary comparisons aside, what every translator aspires to is a finished work that is at once eminently readable and which conveys the emotion and meaning of the original.

The Invisible Presence offers the English-speaking reader the unique opportunity of coming face to face with those voices of contemporary Spanish American poetry which have remained hidden until now. Here are poets whose commitment to their calling is profound enough to have transcended the limitations imposed by the vicissitudes of their time. Let us open this anthology with these words by Aldo Pellegrini taken from his essay "Poetry is everything that closes the door to imbeciles:"[2]

> *"Poetry is a mysticism of reality. The poet seeks to find in words not a means of expressing himself, but a means of participating in reality itself. The poet has recourse to the word but searches in it for its*

original value, the magical instant when the word was created, when it was not a sign, but a part of reality itself. Through the word, the poet does not express reality but participates in it."

(Toronto, August, 1995.)

Notes

[1] Anna Balakian, "The Surrealist Optic of Ludwig Zeller," *Review* 21/22, Fall/ Winter (1977), p.162.

[2] Aldo Pellegrini, *Para contribuir a la confusión general* (Buenos Aires: Nueva Visión, 1965)

Rosamel del Valle

Chile

1901-1965

BIRTH

Open up, open up, open up. I come from the least desperate of hours. A glow exists and it will appear exactly when this noise I struggle with is cut in half, as it happens to twin waves when they abandon the sea. I hear it coming, descending, falling while I carefully remove all manner of earthly breathing. Because I have heard the message and have been told that nothing will be possible if someone lets a word fall on my ear, if an animal suddenly emerges in the night with a torch on its horns, if a bird flies through my chest with a ring on each wing. And while I wait, the world must remain the statue of melancholy. Solitary statue on the beach of an ocean whose waters do not froth up. The statue often visited by an invisible flash of lightning, father of a storm tangled in the forests of a country without name. And how will the eyes rejoice in anticipation when they speak the language of the shadow, bearer of the banquet for the dying man? It is, of course, impossible. Resplendence arrives. Life arrives. The key, walking alone toward the door merely says that it will arrive. The man who unawares pursues me in his dream, which differs from my own, knows only that I expect what is to come. The gathered voice of the earth does away with its frayed garments while it becomes accustomed to the idea that the sun will arrive at last. The threatening sea is now a dragon threatened by the ship, hunter of waves announcing its arrival, its masts are on fire. And it arrives. But I can neither come nor go. Open up, open up, open up. A minute longer and I will not be able to say whether resplendence has indeed arrived, whether or not the hands of light are frozen, whether the day, unknown to me as yet, is or is not similar to the dream I have surrounded it with in order to liberate it from the storm. From the storm which does not resemble death and so resembles nothing: Not even the eye which in vain searches for a way out through me.

(1952)

SECOND LOVE SONG TO THE HEART

We will meet in the descent. Perhaps in the ray of sunlight
That our eyes call the last and our tongues the first,
Because of the way it touches subterranean humidity. Don't wait
For my dissolution. I still roam the prairies inhabited
By what you are. And you may want to know that this dusk
    with drums for tigers
Has not fallen to pieces, almost as you imagined it every day
In your own jungle and in mine. Nor have those clouds hanging
In the distance shifted with the message we never deciphered.
You should not believe that the love you heard in my chest
    like a trombone
Has stopped singing because the earth finally opened.
"Perhaps tranquillity already speaks to you under that whip." Yes,
You may think so. But you know that the language of my sun
Invades the forest and brings old stories back to life.
In case you wish to remember, the trumpets I called tears
Are still alive.

        Why not believe in the pleasure
Of our descent when we follow the traces of the true night?
You say waking up is death and dream is resurrection,
You can say it again and no one will argue. And
The senses will not intervene because you walk a rope
Held to my life. And I would never, no, I would never allow
The weight of a wandering leaf on your astonished gaze.
Nor would the abandoned sun enter your cage
And shine a little longer. No, never. And if I drag myself
With a tangle of clouds around my feet, it is for my own pleasure
As I pull you, step by step, into a sea that grows more distant
Than the iris of your eyes in my dream. I pull you toward
    these instruments
Eager always to say something when guided by the sound
Of your face so often there, beheaded on the pillow.

I have been called the lonesome hunter, perhaps because I placed
My ear next to the earth's body. Perhaps because I follow

The ash that falls from the word of man when he wishes
To resemble the tiger gazing at itself in the water. But then,
Why not praise the ailing sleepwalker for going more often than
the others
Through doors marked by the angel with the lamb's blood?
And who but you has ever invited me to descend into the well
of melancholy?
Magic herbs protect me as I walk down unexpected roads toward
dissolution, your hand in my hand.
No, no warmer ointments exist. No saints, no deeper signals
Exist when you come in, when you arrange the furniture
And decorate the walls of the new home, this cold house
Some wish were the country of death.

No one sees your hand with its only finger, yet they know that
it guides me
Like the fabulous star guided the Magi. I am the beggar content
With its metamorphosis in the night at the doors of the cathedral
Of that inexorable god. Content with keeping the secret while
Others wonder where the wind made of bones is coming from,
Like the last string of the violin set on fire by the bow. With this
Everything resembles the word you don't utter because
nothing is ever uttered
Except in the manner your mouth has of celebrating. Nor is the
devil more ferocious
In the saint's desert than when you smile at the favorite angel.
Maybe the instant the Count of Orgel's stone trembles
To avoid collapsing into the arms of life. An image,
You see. Especially when my soul wants you of stone, of flame
Gathered in the solitude of people who do nothing but to interrupt you
As I am sometimes interrupted in my solitary clock dream.

Only you know that no one gave me this inferno, because I myself
Grabbed it as it went by on a leaf swiftly carried by the wind.
If one must point to the guilty one, here is the smile of my heart
Enraptured as it rots in the pleasure of its own flames.
Because I was the tree that attracted lightning, I was
the secret guide
Of the storm unchained in search of its victim. Without this

I could not have allowed my burning weariness to rest on your
    shoulders
Forever leaning toward the abyss. And love could never be
The vineyard inhabited by lightning. And it would not be possible
    for me
To talk with the smiling worm sleeping inside the fruit.
Ovid would not be here trying to defeat my endless resistance.
Don't forget that in order to please you I am still an insect
Pinned to the wall. This is how I want you to imagine me
Stuck to your heart forever. Only you know how and when
You will give me your sun to rejoice in beautiful death. Any sign
Will serve as your word of love in my suffering. All the echoes
Will remind me that I live on your shoulders, and perhaps I
    will put my ear
To your womb and sobbing I will speak with the child that never
    came.
There, as in the seal of the god that will visit us one day. Joyful
    perhaps
That the demiurge was unable to knit the spider web
And we may be mistaken for Adam and Eve on that pale day.
Oh, no. When I say love, I say love. And with that I set aside deaths
And enter your rejoicing. In the kingdom built by me
While in conversation with the tides. In the sea shaped like a lion
So that love be love and dream be a clamorous wound.

Today I speak to you under a sterile sky gathering
Echoes from caves, the sobbing of solitary angels inside the wells.
You may think this is so. Nothing is new to me. The sea in your eyes
    speaks
Objects hang from your chest at the sound of a fruit. And if I remove
This abyss, it is to shine for one day. To make a new sky
For you and for me. Do you remember how we put our ears to
    the sand
And listened to the dolphins sleep? And "the symphony of
    the solitary dolphin,"
Said the sea, with its way of speaking between its teeth. It is
Like descending on a given day with a cup of tea in one's hand
Into a room where visitors fall apart. "You could
Sing differently to love. You could die differently,

Without the crown which humidity lays on you soul,'' spoke
The sea. And the sea often knows what it says. Just as my heart
Knows how to burn for you at this hour and at any hour.
And when the hour called for our dissolution does come, when your
Head becomes a wandering statue searching for me, on that day
    I will be sitting
For you, to the right of the father of all the winds, with the son
That death will have given us before closing the last door of the night.

(1956)

WRITING

You will live only when followed by invisible threads, tireless bearers of the unique message of a world barely seen. You will not see this life without dying and trying to pass the spectacle will be in vain because it glows no more than the birth of the night and is no more somber than the farewell of the shifting star. You will not forget to place the storm next to the clothes you take off before going to bed since the road that you must walk is long when body and thoughts shed their everyday leaves to enter the water of dreams. And you will try to understand the wisdom of the sun as it tiptoes through the grass for fear of seducing the insects, for fear of separating them from their musical tasks. This is why man's hands allow him to keep his balance while he sleeps. And it could be no less true that the lips of the dead taste of dried hemlock. And this: I. When, during the night one descends into the abyss, it is not worth our while to come back unless comforted by ointments totally unrelated to aromas. II. Man will have his word and will want to hold you by it. If you allow it to pierce your ears, the word will be wise enough to go back to its nest. And you will not forget that it is the name they give to the wasp's home. III. You will live your dreams. An offering not yet received, an order not yet fulfilled. IV. A science: to be truly young. Yes, to be the morning's young death at all times The most beautiful, the deepest of echoes. After all, the lark's song is not always pleasant. But there is always a new sun in the kingdom. Do not forget that a thread is piercing your heart when you wake up. Live, that they may call you darkness.

(1952)

"THINE IMAGE DIES WITH THEE"*

Time, my time is a handful of sand burning in my eyes
In celestial essences the forest grows with lightning
And faith in the transparency of our actions is still the song of exile
The sea tries to break away from the earth, from the star and
    its dying light
Because sounds of disobedience still breathe life into a boneless night
Wing of the bird driving the rain from hill to hill.

The orders of the guardian night are the somber eye of time,
The eye I swim through in the company of a few bonfires
    a few ravings,
A few less than temporal shapes, a few lenient visions,
Unlike the tattoo which life placed on my chest like a beacon,
Or the shadow dissolving between the dew of temptation
    and discourse,
Or the fascinated body traveling minute by minute toward death.

Oh splendor, transparency of uninhabited bones!
What better moon for the voyage? Where an angel more amicable in
    the face of peril?
Everything will be like the night. In its kingdom I will raise the star,
As I raise silence in a glass and raise love in a dream,
And my distant land, is it not the fiery candlestick,
The heart shedding its grain to the wind of the worlds?
I can thus stroll through this walled universe, through this
    flowering space,
Through a land where memories move toward their final
    metamorphosis

Here I have placed a chair of throbbing jasmines for the wise man,
    a card for the saint,
A sun for the blind man, a fire for the mute, a rope for the cripple
A paradise for the hanged man, a flower for the beggar,
    a pillow for the sleepwalker,

*Shakespeare, Sonnet III

A sea for the woman who approaches swimming from the heart
    of night.

Oh forms, images of my time, grains of these sands,
    lives of my deaths,
While they speak of positive things, of insoluble problems,
    of voyages, of returns.
*"This wound is the gaze of a woman; it happened when they
    extinguished the earth and no one noticed,*
*While the dying man drank his tea and the tea was the color of
    his smile."*
Everything in the kingdom, here where memories enjoy exposing their
    roots to the sun
Life places its hands on our shoulders without our feeling them.

Magic. *"For example, I had a tamed star in my garden."*
Coexistence is not an idea, it is an evocation: *"I must have some of
    last year's waves in my head.*
Objectively, in trance." And there is silence, there is a insect in
    our memory, as there are insects in plants. No more no less,
    the hollow which our actions leave behind, the wake
That follows contemplation and follows action, the weariness
That follows the voyage we must undertake at all hours, always
    in passionate company.

*"And the colored things the beautiful lady with magnet eyes was
    saying...*
She was like a Madonna." But there is a river within us, a river that
    goes nowhere,
A river that carries the sun on its back as I carry my solitude from
    one world to another.
And there is a body torn by the years, parched by a dream
    of indestructible love.
Not in me, really, but in my shadow, in the shape of my body
    which resembles an idea,
Total apparition and radiant summer, crown of loneliness
    and mirror of fire.

Time, perhaps the echo of a catastrophe, a lighthouse, perhaps
    the single string
Of a forgotten instrument, the clay cup lost amid magical ruins.
The one sound, the yellow shadow, silent breathing inside the temple,
Night made to measure so that neither you nor I will fit.
"Each one in his hole," is the command of the earth. This is how we
    are left alone,
With no other communication in the end, than the sound of
    the grass and the rain beating down.

(1960)

VISIT

He will come, one thinks, and the visitor arrives. The room opens.
Needless to say, he comes in. The walls lose their tranquillity, objects
lose their tranquillity, the light loses its tranquillity and whatever I am
when I extend my greetings is in no way related to the word tranquil-
lity. I know then that the walls are shaped like an ear and that the
visitor will rest his own on the lock of the door as if to assure himself
that half his thoughts have remained outside, as if to pay tribute to me
in the name of loyalty. It is perhaps for this reason that I remember
his behavior as having always been irreproachable. The moment I
notice him taking off his hat and throw it into the ocean I know that
our conversation has begun. A conversation of humid words, similar
sometimes to summer, sometimes similar to the sweating window
panes. I couldn't say for sure. However, without anything leaving his
mouth he utters exactly what I heard in my dream last night. It is the
story of a conversation never started. Then, to avoid a tragic farewell,
I turn to the wall and give back to the visitor the blank page which
threatens to collapse from its teeth any moment now. And when I hear
the tear falling from the door that closes, tranquillity lights up once
again in the room. But it is late and it would be useless for me to
attempt a walk on the shores of that river which in this instance does
not reach the sea.

(1952)

THE APOSTLES' BAR

Yesterday the wine tasted of irises. When
We remember the moist smell of the earth
Things get complicated. We think of autumn on the earth.
We think that each word carries the color yellow.
Yet every country has an autumn and a color of its own.
   This is how fish
Can stay out of the water for so long. / ''As far as I am concerned
In my heart it rains all year round and I count the drops
As the clock counts the minutes.
The sun can be seen undressing behind glass
And one can hear the earth sobbing as it parches.
Maybe because the hours fall on tides of hair
When we set life on fire.'' / The wine
Tasted of irises.
        ''Yesterday? I remember now, I had
To watch a woman dying on the street. Smoke in her mouth.
Fire grappling time. Of course, no one allows himself
To be caught by the storm. It is difficult to sever a hand thus,
To cut steam into columns of eyes, to sever
Life suddenly, to cut a wild dahlia
By the side of the sunniest road. Difficult.''
Difficult. And death smelled of irises. Difficult.

''I shouldn't play cards today. My heart weighs me.
They placed a stone at the edge. Like following the thread
Of an endless dream. An incredible story.
Much like a wedding. Everyone dressed up as ghosts
Step by step / Isn't that how soldiers come back from war? /
A road of music and irises. In the background, a sound.
They were burying someone. I am sure. I definitely
Must not play cards today.''

     All it takes is to run
One's hand over the moist earth. Everything has gathered
There to sing. The sowing of bones has borne its fruit.
Voices have borne their fruit. The cloud of smoke

Will be higher this year. We are right:
Death smells of irises. "Beloved dew."
Who will not be at the table today? I ask. I could not
Live without asking now that the sky passes by.
A cloudless sky, of course. The alchemist's light,
The magician's mirror. We are so earthly nowadays.

"Just let me remember. A foggy city.
Everyone went by with their hands raised
And the sea came out to greet them." I know. My wound
Had borne its fruit on the sand and the wind opened
And passed into the night. "When that woman slept
On the grass the waves were bells.
How sweet the descent into the kingdom. I still think of a dream
As large as a seed. And that woman
Was sleeping for me. Do you remember?"
                    Sometimes the fog
Prevents us from loving with all our hearts. And how ardently
We love on public walks, perhaps like the animals do
In the Zoo on Sundays. "From my mouth to your mouth
There's a bridge of flames." The cards speak a negative
Language and no one hopes to win. Somewhere
A woman deceives. You should be horrified by the lucidity
With which you set destiny on the table.

"I am not the one who drinks or plays. Once / things seem
So unreal / the devil moved my hand and the abyss
Was honey. I had a hymn inside." Another story.
We shouldn't play around with stories. I say so because the night
Perpetually drowns itself. I should be at home.
Fire burns there because it's the anniversary / for how long? /
Of a death. The memories choke me up. The shade of her eyes
     matched the color
That spreads over the skin of the shipwrecked. Ideas can choke.
The light is so scarce that the knaves get confused with the queens."
Perhaps. But somewhere man is still being pursued
By horseflies. Has another kingdom fallen in the last few days?
Is there more to be done in the sanatoriums? Has a new
God emerged?

"In the garden the butterflies had glass
Wings and a two-headed lily had flowered.
Nature contributes substantially to the anxiety of the times."
Fantastic. The queen's stairs. Luck
Is a toothless old woman. In the past wise men
Were respected. Today they respect the hysterical. Life
Is an old woman with teeth. Sometimes I think
That the sea is under my pillow.

It's too late to go on traveling among echoes.
Let us divide the stone into sobs. "It's late. Here
I will build my new house," says the dying man. It's late.
Divided, let's divide. It's late. In each one of us
It's late. A glass, a letter, an idea. It's
Late. The sky changes places and the sea falls to pieces.
The light cuts through us. We leave, we arrive, we come back.
   The earth
Is a hunting horn in the hills. "Tomorrow
Our hands will be dry." Why light up
The lamps again? It's late.

It's late.

(1952)

BREATHING

After all, what I do is to live without betraying others or myself and I know life better than the one who chooses one for himself to show it off at the public square. I say one life because there are those intelligent enough to furnish themselves with several lives and are apt to take to market the one that best suits the occasion. Does this life have a name? It does, but it is a phenomenon that changes with the sun. That is the purpose of the man we greet each morning. They say it is his blood. Well, my blood does not change color with the sun, nor does it splash. I do what every man with a task must do in order to survive. And I aspire to dream freely. Furthermore, I don't want anyone to die other than his own death and I loathe those who impose death in the name of any circumstance, idea or myth. It is not easy to reach the hierarchy of the worm. Just as it is difficult to get used to putting one's ear level with the earth and live with the terrible love for things that aspire neither to power nor to desire. And don't talk to me about heroes. I would rather believe what the heart of each person does not say. I would rather think of what a butterfly does by night, of the terror each human being finds inside himself when alone. That is to say, the words that our bones utter. I am here. I also tremble. And if I allowed myself to be taken to shout it out at the square, I would not hesitate to start my speech with a ''Let man's heart tremble!'' And yes, I know, they say that trembling is being irresponsible. Need I add that this eternal responsibility they talk about and which I dare not assume resembles that of the worm? May the gifted and the hero forgive me. May everything I don't see forgive me. May everything that shouts forgive me. I have the sea caught in my ears.

(1952)

EURYDICE IS THE FORGOTTEN STAR

We descend into hell between arguments
The most self-assured affirm having learned to converse with fire
And there is someone writing "The Anatomy of Melancholy"
A new Robert Burton this time engaged in conversation with Eurydice
Besides, nobody goes to bed without having eaten a bit of fire
And it would be useless to deny that we part with the world at dusk
"In an island where everyone is named after a tree"
Very spectacular for the times they answer
Incredible, and yet, such is the color of the rain in my country
And when someone discusses the matter it becomes clear that
    they have not understood
A punishment for the ease with which we appropriate things
Perhaps the problem is that everything resembles our lies
Of course the way in which we open our eyes
Is far from satisfactory – hasty at most
While Eurydice is the forgotten star
And will remain so until we have less mist on our tongues
Because no one wants to sit at the table with the night
It seems so wise to prefer a portrait to the eye watching us
    from the wall
They say that it is not fear of death. Do not deny
Your horror of the stone's strange perfume, flower that
The bees look for when they wish to sleep. Do not deny it.
We die today the moment we speak, why argue
About what the comets tell each other when they meet?
Fire has the last word – And when fire speaks
The angels have again set Paradise ablaze
Strange tongues express this forgetting
We've heard something of the sort before
Such curious negotiations are started with secrets

(1956)

VERONICA

Veronica, the shroud on the weary face
Was billowing in the wind. I have seen it again in the streets
Of my city. It was not burning wonderment nor the proof
Terrible, alive there, in the magic net the head they pulled out with the
  catch. It was not the abyss which met those fishermen deprived of
  light. It was not the face growing in the cloth, the face which your
  hands extracted from death's lonely threshold.
I have seen it again. The crown was a little erased and the
Adoring eyes were distant. Distant, perhaps
In an altar, next to the votive lamps. Perhaps in a dream
Of horror for those who did not love him enough. Veronica, that cloth
Was not meant for the face which the fig leaves gathered
For your lovely fingers.
And the crowd, still moist two days after the flood.
And the terrified prophets, the saints with their halos
Falling off their heads, singing a song full of thorns
A song dispossessed of heaven and earth. And you,
You were flowering inside that white tunic,
Still holding your hands in the air, still holding on to the net
And the wounded head. The generous song was opening the way
For that proud dead man. No, the handsome man born again from
  among the living.
Meanwhile, the heavens were tinged with uprooted trees
And the lightning bore inedible fruits.

There was a great winter on those burning beards.
A cut sun inside each mouth. And they sang.
Without a doubt they sang, lead by the magic star
Of love for the one they were killing there, far from the olive trees.
Step by step they went through the city whose stores
Were closed as though it were Sunday. Sometimes the windows
Flaunted crowns of myrtle and suffering voices
As the lugubrious procession made its way. And you, just you
  and the shroud
Over your heart with the one eternal proof, the lantern of stone,
  the face covered in blood, the face pricked on the rose bush,

suddenly drawn to salvation and rustic perfumes.
How could you close your ears to the song? How could you make
    your way among the people
Toward torment, abandoned and blind without the expected miracle
From the Father, silent in the immense sky?

I have been there, Veronica. I have followed the drops
Of pain dripping down your eyelids. I have played the lute
For the dead. I have read the book. I have breathed
The sulfur of the way to the Calvary. Behind you. My heart
Was cutting its roses in silence counting
The thunders that would come at the very hour
Of the deepest death.

Oh, I knew that your forehead wished to return to the catacombs,
To the solace of the ancient stones, to the dampness
Of unguarded fervor. There, where the poor prayed
And grew in an underground garden perhaps, between torches
    and hushed songs whose echo searched for a way to the heavens –
    their voices would carry the flower of the faith in that open heart.
You wanted to return to death. You wanted to
Forget the torment and once more feel the heartbeat of that young
Promised eternity. You wanted to water the dried grass on that chest,
To care for the lamps with the deep oils of your soul, clean the
    entrance. You wanted to look deep into the eyes
Of your brothers and place the leaves of the fig tree
At the feet of the old pilgrims
And once again kiss
The leper's furrowed brow.

But the face went hidden in a bundle of wood
Carried on the back of an ass from the city .
You were the face. You would never have denied him,
Unlike that arrogant apostle. You would have raised in the air
The earthly wound, abandoned sorrow.
What was eternity on that cloth? The wind from
The olive trees, a lonely wind blowing with the eyes of a chimera.
There, next to the sepulcher. The same wind which blows over
    the graves,

Like your hair capable of blowing over our hearts,
Sweep away the dirty leaves and stop the crying
Which rescues nothing.
You, whom I loved despite that cloth,
Despite your love for miracles. You, whose hands I saw
Forever shine and blind the mouth that got too close.
You had a lamp in your heart. I knew it.
We can talk now. I can now say that love
Lead you to the rescue of the wounded face. You wished to
Hold on to the unfortunate image, touch that abandoned eternity.
Who were the ones surrounding him? Those who accompanied him
Were biting at love and at faith. They were following a different
    dead man.
A dead man without a shroud, a dead man
Making his own way to his grave. A light
Cut through your will and followed your hand. You knew
How to guide eternity. You knew that the cloth was a breath
That would waken your simple soul, make a spike out of
    that abandoned solitude. I could see you smiling, smiling till you
    cried before that face, the face waiting for the sky to open, for
    lightning to separate, for the storm to pant. The face of that lonely
    son, sheaf among men and soldiery. Sheaf or earthly stubble for
    earthly love. Sheaf of hell for a terrible hell. And your tears
    brought the rivers to the sea.
The treasure on your chest. A flag, an eternal flag
For your loveless heart. Living lantern in the wind
Which no one saw. Just you, just you, the stranger,
Among the others with your head like a tormented
Bird in mid flight.

Oh, what a sad hour, Veronica. Your soul was waiting
For the sound which the great presence would make when it broke
    the air.
Rainbow of one thousand colors and a black belly
Over the lightning and the storm cut loose.
You were hoping to show that face and find salvation. *"No, I cannot
Perish. No, the punishment is not for my temples. My hands
Held him in that wretched trance. He is here.
He is here. How can his face perish with me?"*

You were waiting for me. A soft wind left your house to glimpse
And looked without seeing. Nothing came. Nothing opened.
New lances were sowed on his side. New tears.
New doubts growing like the old linden trees in the chests
Of the wounded apostles. And in the distance, the crosses,
The open arms. The dark hill. But nothing came.
Nor will anything come. Everything will be done. And the whip grew
Like nettle. And you with your load of light.
You with that cloth in the air.

I have seen you again in the shiny city. There are temples now,
Shiny gold on the domes. The new apostles
Go cheerfully to the banquet, though they wear black. The chalice
Is fresh wine. Bread is a tasty dish. No woman
Envies you your cloth. The organs sing what was not sung.
They still sing to death. We must rejoice. Yes, rejoice in
The good fall, the horrible trance.
And here, on the walls of the cathedrals
The moss grows. Death grows. The forgotten man grows.
And you are not here. You are not like before. You are dressed in
    evening clothes
On your way to the costume ball. You come out of the 1945 Packard.
You wear gloves and a flowered hat. A young apostle
Offers you his arm. The beggars think they recognize you and their
    hands
Shake without coins. The poor think they are seeing you again
When you cross the portal and step sure-footed into the nave.
You are there, kneeling, almost happy to be praying without effort.
The candles are now electric. The rugs would never allow the muddy
    feet of the believers from the catacombs. Peter is wearing a
    Hawaiian shirt. James shines in tails. Paul keeps his tailor busy
    with his growing girth. Judas goes to the game and no longer goes
    to confession on Sundays. Matthew feels nothing but horror at the
    visions.
Your young apostle is yawning. You are not so beautiful
    when you pretend.
He prefers you in bed, burning with abandon.

Veronica, the cloth.

I see you from outside. I do not go in there.
My heart is pure though this eternity clouds it.
I cannot adore the lost god.
I cannot be with those
Who saw the Calvary.
But you are love. What became of that cloth?
The world is in a party mood. The world loves the murdered man,
Loves a terrible death.
No. I want to live. You want to live.
Well, I remember that cloth.
I will see you tonight,
Tonight, when the young apostle
Leaves you on the bed
And goes to pray
In the Olive Grove.

(1949)

Enrique Molina

Argentina
1910

FRANCISCA SANCHEZ

You who come
from remote dark lands.
Ruben Darío

Disguised as ambassador as monkey
As duke from the confines of lust
Nothing extinguishes the constellations of the tropics
The blinding volcanoes
Fermenting full-swollen with flowers
In his heart
– Oh, beloved Rubén!–
And suddenly
The phosphorescent maid is singing down the corridors
Of a Madrid rooming house
Her wild hair touches vertigo's nape
So many nights spent
Wrapped in poisonous shadows
The ghosts propagate they howl
In her terrified blood
In rooms furnished with sleeplessness
Once again she appears naked between monticules
In a landscape she slowly unrobes
While pleasure devours him
His veins fill with living coals
Next to that twin body in the darkness:
Francisca Sánchez
Alone on the grass of caresses
Alone with her burning doubts
The wind reconstructs their laughter
Her wolf-like embrace
Her lips predestined
For this king fascinated by life
Pompous prophet at the edge of catastrophe and glory

Lit by provincial candles
By the bewichment of a remote decapitated hearth

In a corner of Castille
Death's black smoked sausages
Life's red ham
Against the stinginess of the literati the nuptials
The prostitutes and newspapers
She makes the wheels of those
Immemorial breasts turn
She comes back counting
The crabs on the beach
Her peasant legs shine in the rings of the sun

Years and more years
Domestic Yadwige reclining on a sofa in a jungle
Of dark habits and carnal opulence
Fusing root and insanity humbleness and inconsistency
Into fumes of caresses
She loosens her fatal braids
While the warmth of her sleep surpasses
All shelter from stone temperance or pleading
As she grows more tyrannical
As she grows more affectionate
The spiral of her thighs her limitless body
Her sex
Winged slope that reaches down to the last cell
Like the night slowly cauterizing
In places that become dispersed
Barcelona Paris Les Halles La Cartuja Mallorca

A home in the wind
With spoons sheets insults hymns
For the burning guest of temptation
The luxury of a world full of lips and graves
Ignorant like the rain
Francisca Sánchez
Reads into the bread that she cuts in dreams
She reads in the salt of her tears
Archaic wild creature
In a bowl of soup
Dissolves the mind of the dead like an ocean

Warm armpits and tongues
She alone is real
When the milk dawns deep in her eyes
Wretched Rubén
Only she is real in the maelstrom
Of lightning's teeth
When you sob
Under the black cloth which sometimes covers your head
– A beautiful scaffold hood –
You twist you float in the dampness
Of a fortress of rats
– *Francisca Sánchez come with me!* –
                    And in the distance
The oily bay of the parrot
The sun's dignity on the banana trees
The suffering hand of the honeycomb caresses you
While the pearls of death grow
                    And once again
The woman of the birds watches you with sadness
Your clothes obey her and the night
                    Grants you
The savage absolution of her body
Through the furniture of the earth
Carved out of roots
Across the ocean
you can still see her crying
alone against the wall of Spain
made of coarse desert salts of hardened blood

Memory and abandonment

(1966)

HIGH TIDE

When a man and a woman who once loved one another, separate,
the burning song of pride rises like a golden cobra
the illusory wonder of their nights of love
constellations of passion
the fury of their untamed voyage their stone-piercing laughter the
    pleading and the rage
dramas born of secret buried insults
the perverse intrigues the hunting the arguments,
dark human bolt of lightning and the fulminating whiplash of the
    antipodes which held the furor of their bodies for an instant
facts drifting in the gauzy surge of dreams
memory's octopus stares fixedly
an old woman trembles suddenly and the pallor of sadness and all
    the gestures of abandonment shroud her
two or three books and a shirt inside a suitcase
it is raining while a train slides down the frantic mirror of the storm
    tracks
the hotel faces the sea
all those imaginary dwellings all those places never to be reached
the endless bustle of people carrying useless objects people
    dressed in dusty clothes
cemeteries of birds pass by
heads attitudes mountains alcohol and shapeless contraband
each night as you undressed
the shadow of your naked body grew on the walls until it reached
    the ceiling
the enormous wardrobes creaked inside those flooded rooms
unknown doors virgin faces
imprecise disasters bewilderment of adventures
always just about to leave
always waiting for the outcome
with her head resting on the wound
her heart bewitched by the threat of Tantalus over the world

A trail of blood
a submerged continent in whose mouth the spray of helpless days

still boils under the sun's breath
the knot of bodies turned into constellations by the resplendence of
insatiable sequins
lips kissed in other lands by other races on another planet in
a different hell
returning on a ship
the city was coming up to the gunwale dragging its heavy salts like
an enormous Galapagos tortoise
hallucinations lingered on the bridge and the suffering of maritime
work with the throne of waves collapsing with the propeller tree
just under my cabin
this is the excessive world the irreplaceable world a desparate world
like a celebration of hurricane stars
but there is no pity for me
there is no sun no sea the mad pigsty of the ports
is not there wisdom of the night whose song I hear through
the mouths of waters and fields with the violence of this planet
which belongs to us but escapes us
you were there at the end
waiting on that pier while the wind returned me to your arms like a
bird on the prow
they threw the rope with a lead ball at one end and tied it to the cape
of Manila
everything comes to an end
voyages and love
nothing ends
not the voyages not love not forgetting or covetousness
everything wakes up again with the mortal tension of the beast that
lurks inside the sun of its own instincts
everything goes back to crime like a soul chained to happiness
and the dead
everything sparkles like God's pebbles on the beach
lips washed away by the great flood
left behind are
the halo of a lamp a bedroom razed by the vehemence of summer and
the leaves whirling over the empty sheets
once again the claw of fire leans on the heart of its prey
in this confused New World open in all directions
where fury and passion mix with the pollen of Paradise

once again the earth unfolds its wings and burns with thirst
    intact and without roots
when a man and woman who once loved one another
separate.

(1961)

DEAD SERF

The woman crouches inside her attic
She is inside the palest part of things while that long creaking
solitude reaches her hips sheltered by a miserable blanket
    Silence reveals a land too vast
    Forlorn places filled with faces which dawn exorcises
    When she cleans again
    The bronze blood off the gargoyles off the nightmares of the house

Day in and day out she goes sterile sphynx, again and again she
creeps inside that manger dampness where dawn is dripping
    The wind blows deep inside her breasts between the boards
Of her irreversible room dissolving into provincial clouds of dust
    A hare with scarlet eyes jumps out of time onto the grass
of her childhood
    Presence and memory are identical:
    Knives and horses in a town of bitter sands where
the hens are pecking
    The picture of the singer on the wall, native rivers and the pin
made of tin and the glass of her jewels
    The smell of cheap powder the smell of hair at naptime in the
humbleness of resigned bewitchments
    – Oh kingdom in the rain! –
    All that dark desire without novels without contagion
    On her island her shipwrecked darning barely serves as light in that
ocean
    Of courtyards of brooms and utensils and dishes which surround
the pale sceptre of her soul
    Sister to Baudelaire's servant under the wings of every cemetery
    The woman clots between tresses that are a black parenthesis
enclosing her like the history of stones
    Presence and memory are identical:
    The ritual rocking of her flesh her trembling body which once
lived among organs
    And her blue apron forsaken in death's kitchen with the victory of
her bones sparkling in her long legs under the storm

That terrible summer of stones behind the dark shell of her relics
Yet there is something which still glows
In the river mouths of the earth but does not explain that immense
mysterious traveler
Toward which fire of mercy she is headed
Leaving behind a solitary motionless bird hanging in the wind

And now she is wearing the white mask made of lead where time
goes astray
Her thighs, longtime strangers to love now tremble with the foliage
and leave behind the alchemy
Of lips made for devouring each other
Her whole existence is filtered through the mucous membranes of
the night and the sheets are impregnated by the density of her body
By the sobbing after the farewell
Of the one who intercedes between sun and tomb – oh my poor
one – and disappears
Next to her floor mop with its beating cancer
Next to her bucket now filling up with black eternal water

(1966)

PERPETUAL CALL

The women of the railroad tracks and their indifferent wanderings
    like flowers combed by the ivory of oblivion
furtive queens wagered on in unfamiliar rooms
their nomadic tongues light up our hearts while their garments
    dissolve and their innocence makes them possessors of the
    earth their mouths sweat and they burn over the dead
    over jewels and the sun runs down their backs
                    they sparkle!
like the leaping porpoise in the bursting laughter of the tropics

It is just their amnesia sky. It is just their imperceptible breasts behind
    the great rains
slow carnivores suddenly lost in the middle of the station like a
    coastline that curves toward the uncertainty of another breath!

Hotel moons and the indecencies of other races. The same glance can
    serve as solace and threat. Living things whose mercy exalts us
    like a violated host
whose tenderness is as exciting as the scorpion inside the last circle of
    fire.

Oh beautiful teeth of the devils I love! A woman's sun which flees
    toward the root of her blood
while her body touches all the summer leaves all the feathers of
    madness and touches cocks decapitated by the knife edge of her
    presence
                white flame of lost time!

(1961)

NO, ROBINSON

On your island Robinson
covered by the green fur of madness by colossal ferns
by stars by the virginal parrot and a goat crossed by lightning.
All those fevers!
The cave with its tyrannical cask and the rain beating down
    those immense bilges against the palisades of night.
The ocean reaches your waist
and the shadow of your hand touches your wrenching expression
poised on the scarlet bedroom of your childhood
while the troughs reach the other side of the earth

Don't give up now old dog
don't go back with your boiling apple dragging your feathers of dark
    fleeting bird,
with the smell of roots and mushrooms under the light cast
    by the knife
conspiring with the moon's secrets
you play host and abandon the boats to marine saliva
your visions
your surly resplendence when surrounded by the cyclon's valves
the mathematics of the horizon stretch into infinity
with no guitar other than the shipwreck's bonfire lit anywhere
between the reefs and the slow stones of the sunset
cracking with so much sadness
under so many waters

More forlorn than a god
untamed like a child
more resistant than the mountains to the sky that competes
    for your legendary food
oh Robinson helpless fearless and without remorse!
Traces of your solitary soul reach the threshold of your house in York
    while your iodine steps ignore all heirlooms
at midnight you become the nightmare
while the grace of the abyss touches you to the marrow
and you shout against your invisible father and the undertow
    drags away the masts!

It is dawn and the muddy city is drinking the dead milk of faraway
   hearts under the gold of their clothes
but don't turn around
now that the carriage of spores and saurians passes with the warmth
   of a caress
over your creaking island
in the purity of your exile
Why your shouting?
Why your open hand for the rain to beat down on?
Why your black Bible against the Bible of the hair on your chest?
Pray to nothing.
To everything.
Robinson you who own nothing who are without altar: you are
   master of the world!

(1961)

TO SETTLE DOWN

The black race the white race the red race the yellow race:
the only races I know are the violet race the green race and your
    tongue racing to decipher water and fire

I will be rich – you know – with misery and hunger for the rivers
    to run
rich in the mistakes of those without skin of the stone on the head
as rich as patience and mercy made red-hot

I have no mission no family no dialectic other than these mortal pleas
    where the spray of great sunsets dissolves

Obssessed with the furor of a world that whistles like an escaped siren
for every kiss that reaches the soul
for every mouth that feeds on cantharides bread
for every castaway heartbeat which bursts when captured
    by the storm

I will be rich – my love – under the legs of horses and strangled
    by the night contracting on the waves
robbed by the sea's night and by the greediness of caresses
rich until I go mad like and unspeakable intruder caught in the
    many positions of indolence in the blood's deserted spaces
wherever there is cruelty loss power
promises left unfulfilled by the sky

(1961)

PRE-NATAL LIFE

It was my mother's heartbeat
the tom-tom of darkness
the drum above my cranium
in the membranes of the earth.

(The slow canoe of motherhood
the rhythms of journeying foam
silks of tremendous waters
where the huge tropic throbs)

Her ceremony was day and night –
there was no night, no day
only a deep land of sponges
a whole tribe of drums.

The heart of an organic sun,
a hoarse dream of tapestries
I was the magic the idol
in the depths of the mountains

a drum where the constellations
and tides were pounding
blood that had its beginnings
in the wince of the Odyssey

to live inside an egg of flames
mingling the earth and sky
to live in the centre of the world
Faceless passionless timeless

I grew ancient within that sweetness
mine were the astral eyes of moss
I was the seed filled with stars
an obscure terrible power

Your heart, oh my mother,
echoed like the sea

It beat its untamed wings
its insatiable drum of fire.

I kissed your very core
I slept between your dreams
in a region of red feathers
I was your flesh, your exile

the paradise of your blood
the great pledge to your arms
I heard the sun in its flowing
your heart filled with birds.

The drumbeat of adventure
the drum of the vivid moon
earth burning with its cry
and a life unknown.

Outside all was hostile -
frosts, voices, fingernails,
days roses and grapes
wind light and forgetting

(1962)

Translated by Robin Skelton

GEOGRAPHY

Is it a region of drought? There I remain
petrified on the bed of a lake of amnesia.
Missing objects make their appearance.
A tiny woman at the end of a long long street
old men playing at cards a man on horseback
Lamps in cellars light the small dried up town
the ruined mattresses around which the place
incessantly recedes
                            and disappears
Like a tail down a rat hole.

Perhaps the smoke is different there.
Your indestructible presence in uneraseable rains,
scenes of blood transfusions - their great pallor -
and coastal sanctuaries no longer exist.
Nor do the fingernails of robbers,
famous faces (Oh notorious ones...)

Is anyone familiar with mouths creaking like shutters?
Like a dusty wooden stair that leads to a useless place?
And those eyes united by an enormous wasteland
and the light of other centuries...?

(1966)

Translated by Robin Skelton

EN ROUTE

So many days and so many shadows!
So many nights infected
by the memory of other nights
the tattoos of other beaches.

There are roving groups of insomnias
huge serpents of sloth
families that the grasses overrun
pale people that take themselves away

So many locomotives with black wings
in the dementia of other skies!
So many endless fugitive plains
like sand between one's fingers!

There is tomorrow with a bird
There is burial with a priest
There is a letter to nobody
Lodgings that run away

Archaic mothers like a totem
laying a table of oblivion
a loaf soaked by the sea waves
strange fellow diners

and so many heads in flames
prisoners of old histories
as dazzling as the ocean
in the depths of memory.

There is the wind with a feather
a bed without a caress
the golden sounds of summer
the fresh wound of the breeze

There is the hand of stone and shadow
that hunts for huge roots
There is man made of flesh and dream
with the moon of other regions.

There is one who turns his head,
(he is a prisoner of the dead)
and one who sees a far distant woman
when he thinks of an open door

And those poor couples who make love
above the grasses of the stars
intertwining with the shadow
between the shadows of their arms.

There are the sands of discouragement
with pitch-black sunken cities
living cellars that fold up
like enormous carnivorous flowers

And strange foods that yearn for
the passionate hunger of the earth
beautiful foods exalted
by the silence of the stones.

The savage screams of farewell
from the far away coast
the tortured bolt of lightning
the brightness of old days

The mysterious withering
of so much light and breath
with creatures that absent themselves
disguised by time.

And yet I bite the leaves again
I drink the wine I drink the rain
adore once more the sun born
of an undressing woman

The sea returns, a hero
clad in flames and arrows
a grass blade burns and chains
of undergrowth are undone

Lips cross like a river
your body's purest valleys
the tresses of delirium
the nebula of your sex

(Myself, I belong out in the open
the honor owed my kind I claim
and the idolatry due my veins
my defencelessness in the stream)

(1962)

Translated by Robin Skelton

THE GREAT LIFE

An obscure slave of the ocean
chained to a ship's red sun
I polished the plate of the night
and scrubbed the storeys of masts.

I lived in my violent cavern
thundercaps over the mainsail
I polished the steel of the ship
laboring without hope

At night I heard far away
the seething of cruel foam
green manias of the shipwrecked
between the propeller's teeth

The sea's world crammed with claws,
the earth's eternal waters!
The insatiable crewmen
with phosphorescent mouths

A world of gods that crackle
smashed against the rocks
and the long scream of the abyss
in the cellars of the waves

Enormous bubbles unfolded
the bloody smell of the tropics
shoals of ferocious flowers
the sails of the Drunken Boat

And the red hands of the sky
were beating my chest and my mouth
fed with bread of the clouds
with the inward flames of the voyage

Then the magic would spring up
between the cracks of forgetting
ancient deserted beginnings
that my heart brings back to life

The hill's glass of water
the plant's virginity
the light of my mother serving
her soup of Galilee

The grasses' submissive smell
remote as ivories
ephemeral as a bird
in the orgasm of a breeze

Another century's woman
on the soft mist's pillow
carving in dream an amulet
from nothing but a smile

What did they want from me,
those waters, those birds of prey?
The sea slid through my eyes
with salts of tears and ships.

But then so many newly opened
faces defended me
old places that bled their way
through all of the bandages

Objects that once were of use:
an orange in the roadway,
a silent fish hook, an ancient
castaway in a story

Sickness because of the rain,
green parrot, red patio,
a region as weightless as day
in the brilliance of a smile

and the dazzling marshland
filled with the blood from storms
the shapeless mask of the wind
with its green violent wings

A burning sky, a tree without cloud,
innocent fire, unfaithful child,
a wandering loaf with its head to the sun
a country greedy as hands

Immensity on the naked earth
and imaginary peoples
in blurred huts between inlets
around the bright bonfires

and the stowage, the horses,
the peons, fiestas, fields
all a vast world fitting under
the free wings of a bird.

My soul turned to old things
the shade of banana trees
the warmth of being surrounded me
in the glory of the waves.

(1962)

Translated by Robin Skelton

FOOD

Oh meals! Oh mirages!
I settle into extravagant places every day
With a great desire to live
Anonymous eateries that are part of the repertoire of madness
Under the liturgy of ceiling fans and the deafening sirens of the port
– False hotel food that the mirrors multiply –
The tablecloth is always running away burning in the storm
And my eager mouth is covered with red saliva
Like an imperial candlestick
Lighting up the head of the table
– Oh foods! –
The great nutritious host where desire and fire come to nest!
Shaggy salads and helpless
Unlucky stews emerge from every hole
From the very depths of the planet
Surges the eternal murmur of those great devouring mandibles
A likeness rendered slovenly with animals and leaves
The splendor of all of this demented food
Clinging vigorously to my soul
Like a naked woman showing off the moist rays of her sex
A place for the dogs of my blood to share out the sun's heart
Surrounded by the smell of fried things miracles and wines
While I challenge the rattle of the dead
And the diabolical rat glows and makes its way down my life
Insatiable
Without ever reaching a single plate

(1966)

Olga Orozco

Argentina
1920

CHRISTOPH DETLEV BRIGGE

Christoph Detlev's death had reigned over
Ulsgaard for a long, long time
It spoke to everyone, it questioned.

Rainer Maria Rilke: *The Notebooks*
of Malte Laurids Brigge.

The mansion in Ulsgaard was filled with the death of Christoph
Detlev Brigge.
Only with his death.
He did not drink death's poison by the spoonful,
it did not reach his chest ambushed in the growing shadows of the
pine trees:
He carried his death in his blood,
burning galleries whose mirrors announced the promised queen.
One day she came to him as the mad wife.
Sixty days and sixty nights bear witness to the furious wedding
at Ulsgaard,
love's lament rose like a howl,
a retinue of dogs and the servants tearing at the mist of the
nuptial gauzes.
The tide and its boiling rage brought down the objects that survived,
stuck like limpets to destiny's skin.
Was there anyone the bells did not summon to the betrothal?
Was there anyone left who did not fear being taken away by the death
of Christoph Detlev Brigge?
The mansion knows.
The march of the newlyweds echoed from one wall to another
as time retreated past each enclosure putting out its finery.
Finally it reached the last room where life,
like a rejected lover, hides the crystals of its shattered face
between its hands.
Everything was concluded.
Now, only the death of Christoph Detlev Brigge wanders in
the mansion, wrapped in imperial banners.

POETRY, DENSE VEILS SHROUD YOU

I do not look for you in the volcano under this deceitful tongue,
I do not look for you in the blue froth that boils and crystallizes
    inside my head.
I search for you in regions that change places when we name them
as I name the secret
and the undecipherable colonies of another world.

Nights and endless days with my eyes wide open under an
    unbearable blinking sun,
looking out for a signal in the sky,
the shadow of a bright eclipse over the face of time,
a white fissure like a slash of God on the walls of the planet.
Something with which to set fire to the dispersed syllables of a lost
    code
to read on these stones the hidden side of my body.

But no Whitsun descends over me with its burning wings.
Variations of smoke,
remains of darkness with masks of lead,
nameless meteors that rob me of my vision between doors knocking.

Days and endless nights locked in the fortifications of this skin
digging into this blood like a mole,
shifting the bones about, shifting foundations and tombstones
in search of a sign, a talisman to reverse my vision, my fall.

Where does the seed of my unspoken words lie buried?
In what part of the current lies the Delphi
from which the voices are set free like a vapor that rises and
    becomes manifest in my voice?
And how will I grasp the drifting sign
– this one and not another –
whose flesh must enter each fragment of this immense silence?

There is no answer that can burst like the constellations do among
    nocturnal tatters.

They are only ghosts that can not be sounded out in the depths,
territories that adjoin the swamps,
splinters of words and stones that dissolve in insoluble nothingness.

And yet,
now
or sometime,
I don't know.
Does anyone know?
Perhaps
through the double thickness that blocks the exit
dangling by a centuries-old mistake caught in the nets of an instant
I thought I saw you emerge like an island,
perhaps like a boat sailing the clouds, in a castle where someone is
    singing,
or a cavern making its stormy way and lit by all its supernatural fires.

Oh severed hands,
the eyes that dazzle and the ear that deafens!

A handful of dust, my words!

(1979)

48

OLGA OROZCO

From this heart I, Olga Orozco say the world that I am dying.
I used to love solitude, the heroic endurance of all faith,
idleness wherein strange animals and fabulous plants grow,
shadows cast by a grand time spent surrounded by mysteries,
    hallucinations,
by flickering candles that go out at dusk.
My story is in my hands and in the hands of those who tattooed my
    hands.
All that is left of my time here is magic and ritual,
dates that the breath of a merciless love wore away,
the distant smoke of the house we never entered,
a few gestures scattered among the gestures of those who never
    knew me.
The rest will be fulfilled in forgetting.
Misery is still carving the face of the one who searched for herself in
    me like a mirror of smiling prairies.
You will find her strangely foreign:
she is my ghost condemned to my form in this world.
She would rather keep me confined to disdain, to pride
for one last fulminating instant, like lightning
and not to this uncertain tomb where crying and hoarse I raise my
    voice
to the whirlwinds of my heart.
No, this death brings neither rest nor greatness.
I can not go on looking at it for so long as though it were the first
    time.
But I will go on dying until you die
because I am your witness before a law deeper and darker than
those ever-changing dreams,
there where we write the sentence:
"They are dead now.
They chose themselves for punishment and forgiveness, for heaven
    and for hell.
Now they are a stain of dampness on the walls of that first room."

(1951)

HOSTAGES OF ANOTHER WORLD

To Vincent Van Gogh, to Antonin Artaud,
to Jacobo Fijman.

The pact was signed in the blood of all our nightmares.
Simulation of dreamers gnawing at the dangerous bone of insomnia.
No trespassing.
Only the saint knew the password to the tunnel and to flight.
The others knew gags, bandages and punishment.
They were there to obey the guards' orders which rose from the
bottom of the well.
Forced to appropriate the plantations that stretch out of sight
    from under
Their feet, in the dark, feel out the walls that separate guest
    and pursuer.
These were the rules of the game in that closed room:
bets left unfinished until the key was lost,
doors that open when death's last die is cast.
But in one leap they reached the end ahead of the others
with their tall crowns.
They burned the heavy curtains,
they pulled the trees in the forests out by the roots,
they tore deep into the membranes in order to get through.
I was a sacred spark in hell,
the gusts of a sky buried in the sand,
the head of a god collapsing between lightning and thunder.
After that, there was no more.
Nothing beyond the flames, the dust, the clamor
forever the same at every turn.
But the hand that was ensnared in the trap brushed eternity,
the pupil that was shattered by the light turned into fragments of the
    sun,
and for a brief moment the broken syllables in that mouth were the
    word.

They were hostages of another world, the car of Elijah.
But they were here,
falling
undone.

(1979)

TO MAKE A TALISMAN

All you need is your heart
the spitting image of your demon, of your god.
Scarcely a heart, a crucible of embers to be adored:
Just a helpless heart in love.
Leave it outdoors
and the grass, howling its lament like a mad wet-nurse,
will keep it from going to sleep
there, where wind and rain crack their whip like a blow of blue
    shivers.
Never turning it into marble, never splitting it in half,
darkness will open its burrows to the packs of hounds
and the heart will not forget.
Throw it down from the height of love into the boiling mist.
Set it to dry on the stone's deaf lap
and dig, dig into it with a cold needle until you root out every last
    grain of hope.
Let the fevers, the nettles, let them stifle the heart,
let the ritual trotting of vermin shake it down,
allow the insults, the shreds of past glories to envelope it.
One day, before it is too late
before the year imprisons the heart in century's claw,
before it becomes a dazzling mummy,
one by one open every one of its wounds,
and expose them to the sun of mercy like the beggars do,
let it grieve its madness in the desert,
until the fury of hunger makes the echo of a single name grow inside it
like the unceasing blows of the spoon against the empty dish.

If it still survives,
if it comes this far as the spitting image of your demon or your god,
here is a talisman more inflexible than the law,
stronger than the weapons and the ill will of your enemy.
Keep it in the wakefulness of your chest like you would a sentinel.

But keep vigil with it,
that it may grow within you like the bite of leprosy.
Your executioner perhaps?
Innocent monster, insatiable guest at your death!

(1962)

NEITHER DOG NOR WOLF

They shut me into myself.
They split me in half.
Day by day they breed me inside patience,
inside a black creature that roars like the sea.
They proceed to cut me out with the scissors of nightmares
and I fall into this world with half my blood on each side:
a face carved deep within by the fangs of fury,
alone, while another face dissolves into the mist of the great herds.
Who rules here?
I decree the plague and with my sides ablaze I cross the plains of
    future and past.
I lie down and gnaw at the little bones of all those dreams that died
    among heavenly pastures.
My kingdom is in my shadow and it follows me wherever I go,
it collapses in ruins, leaves the doors open to the invading enemy.
Every night I tear with my teeth at the ropes encircling my heart
and dawn finds me with my cage of disobedience on my back.
When I devour my god I wear his face under my mask
but at the fountain of men I only drink the velvety poison of pity
    which scrapes at my insides.
I have etched the tournament on both sides of the tapestry
I have won my scepter like an animal exposed to the elements,
and I have also granted shreds of gentleness as trophies.
But, who wins in me?
And, who defends my solitary bastion in the desert, the sheets of
    dream?
Who is gnawing at my lips, slowly and in the dark, with my own
    teeth?

(1962)

MISS HAVISHAM

*Once destruction is complete and they are
dead, they will lay me down on the
wedding table dressed in my wedding
dress.*

Charles Dickens, *Great Expectations.*

Here lies Miss Havisham,
luxurious vanity of disillusionment.
One day, for the sake of happiness, she unknowingly put on her
    death dress .
At the precise hour when she was reaching the music of dream,
someone cut off love's deceitful strings with a hard blow:
released, she fell into darkness like a broken cloud.
Everything was brought to a close.
Do not enter the grounds where a hollow bride once gathered the
frost-covered pieces of her heart for the sake of hate .
The one who entered had been chosen to blindly expiate
    all the crying.
The seals were not to be broken.
The hands of light had dispersed the floating garments,
the tablecloths were eaten away by tenacious dynasties of insects,
the mirror's waters remained murky even after the last image fell,
deserted places where the guests were fallow mourners
sitting around an exhumed woman,
a wilted bride fosforescent still with vengeance and disdain.
Now she is dead.
Come in.
This is the scene kept under the proud dust of patience for
    so many years,
this is the sumptuous warp on which she fell like a tapestry wrapped
in the flames of her own death.
What a splendid bonfire it was!

Yes. Nothing feeds a fire better than vain aridity,
that dark hell where she will burn eternally,
until Pip comes back and writes under her name: "I forgive her."

(1951)

THE SUBMERGED CONTINENT

Odd head,
only partially visible from all vantage points
and only partially rescued from its endless exile in the mist.
Opaque on the outside,
impervious to baptism by light,
like a sponge, porous to the distillations of an insoluble night.
Shiny from the inside and burning
in a whirlwind of wandering crystals
and sparks that leap out of dream's forge.
Whirlwinds of blue vertigo assert that this is heaven's grave.
Believed to have once been a piece detached from God
taking on the form of darkness
rolling down, no doubt cut off by the snake's condemnation.
How many millenia and metamorphose? No one knows.
Nor do we know how many layers of stupor it had to
    cross before it arrived here,
turning like the mole's shadow twisting at the root,
moving forward like a blind planet
that condenses into smoke, into steam, into eclipses.
They inhaled it upward,
and propped it against a tree trunk set adrift and barely able to hold it.
Its two deaf caves listen to the voice that breaks against the wall,
two vain grooves in the cloister allow it to observe the fall,
smelling like an animal cornered under its skin,
tasting like bread buried between fasts,
and this insatiable tongue
which devours the language of death in great bursts of flame.
Stormy head,
indecipherable head,
pensive head:
it resembles a circular hell
where pursuing man becomes man pursued,
always behind itself, or before me,
I, who know not where I come from, clinging to this neck,
never finding the knots that tie me to this strange head.

(1974)

THE GARDEN OF EARTHLY DELIGHTS

Is it no more than a zone of abysses and volcanoes in full eruption, blind, predestined to ceremonies for our species in this inexplicable voyage toward the bottom? Is it a short-cut, a dark ambush where the devil inhales innocence and seals his sentence with blood and fire on the lineage of his soul? Is it simply a region marked as the crossroads for meetings and separations between two bodies that resemble the sun in their submissiveness?

No. It is not a protected climate for the perpetuation of life, nor is it the forge of original sin. And it is not a trap set by instinct, despite the exasperated wind spreading smoke, combustion and ashes. It is not a place, even if the heavens hurl themselves down, even if there is a sky as fleeting and infinite as instantaneous paradise.

Alone it is just a senseless number, a fold in the membranes of absence, a bolt of lightning buried in the garden.

Desire, the surprise of love and the sirens of the voyage are enough and everything is like a tense knot around the senses and the multiple branches that reach out and touch the tree of original temptation and the garden of delights with its secret science of loss spreading suddenly from head to toe as the smile spreads like a net of anxious filaments ripped out of a bolt of lightning, the crisped current crawling in search of extermination, an exit, slipping inward, dragged along by sortileges, tentacles of a sea that pulls with untold vertigo at the root of touch toward the endless center which bottoms out as it falls upward, while it goes through, while it pierces the organic night, questioning, made of crests and snouts and horns, the panting of a fugitive beast, the whip of an unreacheable horizon lashing out at its sides, its eyes open to the mystery of a double darkness, they bring down the planet's hazy machinery with each jolt, they place lip-like corolla in suspension, they are circles that palpitate like fruit, bubbles where the froth of another world beats, constellations extracted alive from their native meadows, the exodus of galaxies that resemble feathers that turn madly in the great flood, in that thundering whirlwind rushing through the funnel of death with the universe in full expansion, with the universe contracting as the sky gives birth,

suddenly making the flask explode, dispersing creation in blood.
Sex, yes,
or its measure:
one half of desire barely equals one half of love.

THE WRONG SIDE OF THE WEFT

With difficulty,
like an amphibian trying to adapt to all the follies of this planet,
with this bread I absorb the masked, insoluble penury of food.
My skin is barely able to dress the boundless sphinx that inhabits me.
My head is small,
yet it holds rooms large enough to fit several cities in its fragile attic.
My hands can't seize the visions that pass through my eyes
nor do my feet touch bottom in my heart's boiling quarry.
And the savage fissure between my tongue and the labyrinths
    of language!
Almost all of my being is invisible,
folded into a blade of grass,
submerged in the mud of immense smallness.
St. Peter's tonsure shining through the keyhole:
Byzantium in a tear.

Daughter of confusion and darkness,
I move forward with difficulty with my load of constructions and
    shipwrecks:
Foolish Caryatid bearing her Olympus on the cloud within,
loosing her minuscule ego as she bumps along like a pebble from the
    great frieze,
a tiny fragment of eternity which rolls toward the world's confines
and gathers herself as she gropes along, without ever reaching her
    place, her destiny.

I praise you all the same with your lack of proportion, with
    your disorder,
incredible existence,
as though you were my body's perfect fit, the exact weight
    of my voice.
And yet, you repudiate me when I provoke,
absurd life among shadows,
like a child intruding in this kingdom,
in vain I question your impenetrable face made of steel and walls.

You turn against me,
you build yourself up, guardian of the sanctuary that you removefrom
    my feet,
you snatch me up in a black hurricane where the tables of the law
    break,
and you leave me in the air, hanging from the edge of orphanhood
    and catastrophe,
while scenes and lands come off the wrong side of my weft
and fall swiftly into the void unfurling their curtains into nothingness.

Everything is possible at that point,
everything, but me.

(1979)

César Moro

Peru
1906-1956

YOU ARRIVE AT NIGHT WITH FABULOUS SMOKE IN YOUR HAIR

You appear
Life is certain
The smell of the rain is certain
You are born with the rain
And with the rain you knock at my door
Oh tree
The city the seas you sailed,
The night opens to your steps
The heart comes back from a distant place leans out
Touches your forehead
And sees your sparkling magic
The mountain of gold of snow
Watches you it sees the fabulous smoke in your hair
And sees the beasts of the night in your eyes
And your body made of burning embers
You water portions of the night
Blocks of night fall from your hands
And silence grows roots when you arrive
And the upheaval and the waves
And houses that sway
Fluctuating lights and a harder shadow
Your words are river traffic
No sooner do you arrive than you are gone
And you want to set my life afloat
But you merely prepare my death
And the death of waiting
And my dying knowing that you are far away
And silences and waiting for the time
When I feel alive because you come back
And you surround me with your shadow
And you make me luminous
And you plunge me into the phosphorescent sea where your existence
    unfolds
Where you and my dark frightful notion of you engage in dialogue
Star cast off the apocalypse

Between the bellowing of tigers and tears
Of pleasure the eternal moaning and the eternal
Search for solace in the rarefied air
I wish to imprison you in
In order to roll down the slopes of your body
And reach your sparkling feet
Reach your feet which are twin constellations
In the terrestrial night
Which follows you chained and mute
Your blood climbs like ivy
It holds your head like a flowering dark crystal
An aquarium which contains planets trailing comets
Power that keeps the world on its feet and the oceans in steady
    balance
And your brain made of luminous matter
And my endless adherence and my love being born incessantly
Wrapping itself around you
Traveled by your feet
As they leave indelible traces
Where we read the history of the world
And the future of the universe
And the luminous binding of my life
To your existence

(1938-1939)

LOVE LETTER

I think of the anguishing holothurians that often surrounded us
    at the nearing of dawn
when your feet warmer than nests
burned in the night
in a glowing blue light.

I think of your body making sky and supreme mountains from the bed
I think of the only reality
with its valleys and shadows
moisture marble and black water mirroring all the stars
in each one of your eyes.

Was your smile not the echo of that forest in my childhood?
Were you not the source
the stone destined centuries ago for me to rest my head?
I think of your face
motionless ember source of the milky way
and this immense sorrow driving me madder than a beautiful
    chandelier swaying over the sea.

Unbearable when I remember you the human voice seems
    intolerable to me
always the vegetal murmur of your words isolates me in this
    total night
here where you shine with a blackness blacker than the night.
All idea of black is insufficient to express the long hooting
    of black on black
glowing fervently.

I will never forget.
But who speaks of forgetting
in the prison where your absence leaves me
the solitude where this poem abandons me
in the exile where each hour finds me.

I will not wake up again
I will no longer resist the onslaught of great waves
that come from the joyous landscape that you inhabit.
Outside in the cold of night I walk
on that board placed above us from which we fall flat.

Stiffening under the terror of successive dreams and shaking
    in the wind
years of dream
aware of what will be found dead
at the threshold of deserted castles
at the place and time agreed upon but never found
in the fertile plains of paroxysm
aware of the only objective
I will use all my powers to spell
that name once adored
and will follow its hallucinatory transformations.
A sword now pierces an animal
and a bleeding dove falls at my feet
which have become coral rock support for the remains
of carnivorous birds.

A repeated scream in each and every empty theater when the inde-
scribable show is about to start.
A thread of water dancing on the red velvet curtains
before the footlights.
Once the orchestra seats have disappeared
I amass treasures of dead wood and hardy leaves of corrosive silver.
No longer content with clapping they yell
a thousand mummified families make the passing of a squirrel
    seem evil.

Beloved decoration where I saw a fine rain balancing itself racing
swiftly toward the ermine
of a pelisse forgotten in the heat of a fire at dawn
trying to direct grievances to the king
I open the windows wide over the empty clouds
imploring darkness to drown my face
to erase the indelible ink

the horror of dream
through courtyards abandoned to this pale manic vegetation.

In vain I ask thirst from fire
in vain I wound the walls
in the distance the precarious curtains of forgetting fall
exhausted
before a landscape twisted by the storm.

(1942)

THE SCANDALOUS LIFE
OF CESAR MORO

Scatter me in the rain in the smoke of torrents that pass
Beyond the night where we meet each time they draw aside clouds
That reveal themselves to the eyes of lovers when they leave
Their sturdy castles whose towers of blood and ice
Tinge the ice and rip through leaps of belated returns

My friend the king brings me to the side of his royal real grave
Where Wagner guards the door with the faithfulness
Of a dog gnawing at the bone of glory
While intermittent divinely mournful rains
Gnaw at the hairdo of the flying streetcar of relapsed homicidal
Sea horses that travel the sublime terrace of apparitions
In solemn carnivorous and bituminous forests
Where strange wanderers get drunk with their eyes wide open
Under great catapults and elephantine heads of cattle
Suspended in Babylonian Trasteverian fashion
The river that crowns your earthly apparition overflows the mother
Precipitates furiously it is a lightning bolt over the vestiges of the day
A deceitful heaping of medals harquebus sponge
A winged bull with significant happiness bites the breast the dome
Of a temple emerges from the ignominious light of day from the
  middle of rotten weightless branches the forest's hecatomb

Scatter me in the flight of migrating horses
In the alluvium of ash that crowns the longevous volcano of day
In the terrifying vision that follows man as the most wonderful
  of noon hours draws near
When boiling dancers are about to be decapitated
And man grows pale at the feared suspicion of the definitive
  apparition which carries the oracle between its teeth and reads as
  follows:

"A razor over the cauldron slashes a brush with bristles of ultra
sensitive dimensions. As daytime draws near the bristles grow until
they touch the sunset. At dusk the bristles turn into a cottage of

humble and rustic appearance. Over the razor flies a falcon devouring an enigma in the shape of condensed steam; sometimes it is a basket filled with the eyes of animals and love letters written in one letter. At other times, an industrious dog devours a cottage lit from within. The surrounding darkness can be interpreted as an absence of thought brought about by the invisible proximity of a subterranean pond inhabited by turtles of the first magnitude."

The wind starts to blow over the royal grave
Louis II of Bavaria wakes up surrounded by the rubble of the world
And comes to visit me while dragging a dying tiger
Through the surrounding forest
The trees fly and become seeds and the forest disappears
And covers itself in creeping mist
Myriads of insects now freed deafen the air
As the two prettiest tigers in the world pass by

(1938-1939)

FIRE AND POETRY

*The burning sun reflects the zenith's hand
on the golden water.*

I

I love love
On Tuesdays but not on Wednesdays
I love the love of disunited states
Love some two hundred and fifty years old
Under Judaism's noxious influence over the monastic life
Of sugar birds of hay the ice the alum the pocket
The love I love has a bloody face and two immense doors that
    open into the void
Love appearing in two hundred and fifty installments
    over a five year span
Love of fragile economy
Like an expansionist country
Which spreads over thousands of naked people treated like animals
To obtain the simple arms of a love
Where crime can stay out all night and drink the clear water
Of the day's warmest blood

2

I love a love of thick branches
Wild like a jellyfish
Hecatomb love
And diurnal sphere over which the absolute spring
Swings spilling blood
A love made of rings of rain
Of transparent rocks
Of mountains that fly and dissipate
That turn into tiny pebbles
Love like a stabbing

Like a shipwreck
The complete loss of our breath's ability to speak
A kingdom of thick shadows
With protruding killer eyes
Longest saliva
Anger at getting lost
Frenzied waking in the middle of the night
Under a storm that keeps undressing us
A faraway bolt of lightning transforms the trees
Into firewood of hair which utters your name
Days and hours of eternal nakedness

3

I love the fury of losing you
Your absence riding the horse of time
Your shadow and the idea of your shadow
Cast over a landscape of water
Your kestrel eyes in the hands of time
Which undoes me and recreates you
Time which dawns when I come out of dream
Leaving me more alone than an antediluvian animal lost in the
shadows of time
Like a toothless beast running after its prey
Like a kite in the sky evolving with clockwork precision
I see you in a thunderous jungle and I loom over you
Fatal like a dynamite bomb
I distribute your veins over me and I drink your blood
I struggle against the day that tears dawn apart
I undo the body of death
And time finally belongs to me
The night catches up with me
And the dream that annuls me devours you
And I can assimilate you like a ripe fruit
Like a stone on a sinking island

4

Slow waters slow road slow accidents
Descending suspended in mid air slow wind
Slow step of slow time
Night does not end and love slows down
The legs cross slowly knotting and growing roots
The head falls the arms rise
The bed's sky the shadow slowly falling
Your dark body like a waterfall slowly falling
Into the abyss
And we turn slowly in the warm air of this hot room
Nocturnal butterflies resemble large sheep
It would be easy to slowly destroy each other now
To slowly tear out our limbs drink each other's blood
Your head turns your legs envelop me
Your armpits and all their hairs shining in the night
Your naked legs
At just the right angle
The smell of your legs
The slowness of perception
Brandy slowly lifts me up
The very brandy that is born of your eyes and which
Will make your shadow grow
Tearing my hair out I slowly rise
To your animal lips

5

Slow waters pour out the days
A head of hair golden sand
A volcano which goes back to the source
I watch you and I count the hours
Time's back is divinely covered with wounds
A naked amphora cleaves the water
Dew confines your body
To the secret regions of a magic mountain

Covered with doll's shoes and visiting cards of the gods
Asmodeus Nero Caligula Agrippina Louis II of Bavaria
Anthony Cetina Caesar
Your name appears intermittently
Over an immense roll of dough
It fills the entire horizon sometimes
Other times it peoples the sky with tiny bees
I can read it from any direction
As it grows and becomes confused with all the words that follow it
When it is an immense piece of light
The furtive passing of the beasts in the forest
A spider slowly dropping onto my head
Or a furious alphabet

6

Slow water slow minimal variations
Slow weightless face
A sigh carelessly cut
The tiny stones
The imperceptible mountains
The water slowly falling
Over the world
Next to your flaming kingdom
The space behind the walls
And nothing beyond this great navigable space
The room rises and falls
But the waves do nothing
The dog observes the house
The wolves retreat
Dawn stalks us it delivers the blow
Blind sleep
The tree has grown taller
I close the windows in vain
I watch the moon
The wind has not stopped calling at my door
A dark life is about to begin

(1938-1939)

THE MOVEMENTS OF MAN

Delirious with pleasure anguished dream drips under the
    lamp we switched off
A horse made of steel emerges from an armor of snow
    with wide open eyes
Dream and rainbow come face to face and tear speech apart
    word by word
The curve that they draw will not be an abandoned slope
    or a living shadow
The cold overwhelms everything because movement keeps its word
A pledge to suit greatness
A low sun a wandering star a tear that shifts places
Movement's delirious pleasure flays the walls of space

In order to live at its own expense the air gets drunk on itself
Oh night
Be kind to the traveler whose sadness breaks the mountains

(1939-1941)

OUT OF SIGHT

I will never renounce the insolent luxury the sumptuous wantonness of
    hair like the finest of faces hanging from strings and sabers
Immense landscapes of saliva with little fountain pen cannons
Saliva's violent sunflower
The word designated the object at hand by its opposite
The tree like tiny lamp
The loss of one's faculties and the acquisition of madness
Aphasic language with its intoxicating possibilities
Nervous ticks anger interminable yawning
Stereotypy long-winded thinking
Stupor
Stupor with crystal beads
Stupor with crystal breath with branches of coral with bronchi and
    with feathers
Underwater clear stupor slipping fire pearls impermeable to laughter
    like duck feathers before the eyes
Stupor leaning to the burning left to the right with its rag columns of
    smoke up the center behind vertical stairs on a swing
Mouths with sugar teeth and tongues of petrol which are born again
    and die and unhook crowns over opulent breasts bathed in
    honey and sour bunches and the variables of saliva
Stupor theft of stars clean hens carved into rock and terra-cotta and
terra firma the length of the eyes
Stupor young pariah of fortunate height
Stupor the women sleep on mattresses made from the rinds of fruit
    crowned with fine naked chains
Stupor of the eve's trains picking up eyes scattered over prairies
    every time the train flies by and silence is unable to follow the train
    which trembles
Stupor like a picklock tearing down mental doors dilapidating water's
    stare and the stare that is lost in the shady side of dried wood hairy
    Tritons protect a woman's shirt while she sleeps naked in the forest
    and walks a prairie confined by mental processes which have not
    been well defined while she endures interrogations answers from
    ferocious stones out of control bearing in mind that the last horse
    died at the birth of the dawn of my grandmother's lingerie while

my grandfather growled as he faced the wall

Stupor the chairs fly to meet an empty barrel covered with
impoverished ivy the flying attic's neighbor asks for the lace for a
drain for the irises of primary shawl while a violent woman pulls
up her skirt and reveals the picture of the Virgin escorted by pigs
crowned with triple crowns and bicolor bows.

Midnight is shaving its left shoulder over the right shoulder grows a
pestilent yet rich grass in agglomerations of tiny prophetic
sheep vitamins painted with trees and cool parasols with fringe and
curls

Forget-me-nots as well as heavier geraniums spit our their misery

Grandiose northern sunset of schizophrenic thinking

Sublime delirious interpretation of reality

I will never renounce the primordial luxury of your vertiginous fall oh
diamond madness

(1938-1939)

THE ILLUSTRATED WORLD

Like your non existent window
Like the shadow of a hand on a ghostly instrument
Like your veins and the intense journey undertaken by your blood
Equally and with the precious continuity which ideally guarantees
    me your existence
At a distance
In the distance
Despite the distance
With your forehead and your face
And your entire presence but without your eyes closing
And the landscape born of your presence when the city was not
    could be no other than the useless reflection of your hecatomb
    presence
To better moisten the feathers of birds
This rain falls from great heights
And locks me alone within you
Inside you and away from you
Like a road fading into another continent

(1938-1939)

Enrique Gómez-Correa
Chile
1915-1995

I GO IN AS SPARROW HAWK
AND COME OUT A PHOENIX

In the night I uncork the bottle and I am a bird
Questioning its own soul
The wave rises
And for an instant the air is but two embers
Seated next to me and fascinated
She follows the light
Of what is and what could be
She cuts nebulae into halves
Which are two enormous feathers.

She loves mystery and sings to hardness
She knows that horror is humming in her ear
And that in order to make two days out of one night
Is as easy as turning
Into a platypus.

You are the ghost in love with purity and you sing
To the dancers
A wall answers you with a ''yes''
More beautiful than a body sown with teeth
You fill your pockets
And get ready for pleasure.

Now you are the growing eye
Which the sea throws on the shore after the shipwreck
Imagine the eye
Threatened by a bulldog's teeth
At that point I would be no more than the flame
Which my Portuguese
Sought in the water,
In the air and maybe even in fire
But they got lost in the frozen cities of dream
And then woke up twelve inches away from my own soul.

It is there that you look for yourself and beat your brow
You see the sky
The clouds are a propitious
Moss for a flock of starlings.

You crossed the vaults of time
You became one with lightning
You swore to sell your soul to the night
You are the flaming wing of the damned
You who know the charms and delights of the night
You were crying before the origin of tears
Now point and shoot all your revolvers into the sky and into
    weariness
Because even thus
My soul, you are a bit less than me.

(1945)

THE WOLF SPEAKS TO HIS DOGS

Look at me: I am incredible like the night
Perhaps because hyenas in larvae state
Have descended on my brain
And have remained
Inside those sad childhood stories
With the fury of the man who
Out of pride makes the air more breathable

We are lost with our friends
In the same putrefaction
We laugh
We abandoned our brides
To a feast of slaughtered dogs
Clouds of love clouds of night
Send me back to the burning faculae of my dreams
In this manner I will not hear the noise
Of the curse that rises to my lips
And will become something blacker than calumny.

(1942)

SPECTER OF LOVE

Ravings have awakened my senses
And I have seen a woman of sumptuous ugliness
Defending herself against
The man with the sparrow hawk feather

The scarce few walls fell
As though razed by light
And the man was tall from the inside
His cranium was devoid of flesh
And his beautiful teeth denounced his victim

The most beautiful page of love was being written there
Night after night the waters divided with great fury
Exposing cities
That had been painted with honey
Destined to be devoured by the stars

The woman – light or darkness –
Was here
Victim of the lime flowing from the eye
Although several sexes
Ran in her blood
And spoke to her of her impossible love
From a man who was tormented
By a great forest

The temperature kept rising,
And by exposing myself to its vapors
I was finally able to reach that free zone of my feelings
Where she remains the unforgettable one.

JEAN ARTHUR RIMBAUD

As the light silently made its way up the arm
Herds of panthers surrounded the hidden regions of the eye
An eye we were familiar with:
It had fermented twenty leagues around us
In the white putrefaction of stagnating waters.

Divine imbeciles were using the same ear to listen to the gun shots
Perfect voices divided into many embers
Only their stems could touch those fingernails
Gladioli victims of sad aquariums

They learned about their backs through mournful wine drinking
Through winds denied them by the angelic
Miraculous tortures of plants by perfumes
That begged for shade from the pavement

This is how they turned red with celestial nothingness
With the angels' troubled vinegar
But without water lilies without kites or pearls
Without the acidity of their cork teeth

Outside communicating temples passed by
Tall crests folded the pupil
They renounced the corolla in favor of the kingdom
In order to produce angel or demon in the midst of battle

In the meantime large bonfires were being lit in Paris
Crabs were surrounding transparent tombs
Blood became paralyzed inside the mouth
Like hawthorn in the hands of the dead man

They knew that
Mist could burn the tips of their eyelashes
In Paris in 1871

They spat the city into the rubble of the sky
The very sky we once so loved
While mouths were being tortured in the same palinode

He went from one set of stairs to the next
Took one thousand blue leaps
In order to feel the light penetrating
The stones
And the vivid color of the tides

Others blended their gestures
Into sea lions cut their fingers
The lunules were ripped out with brute force
While the wind fermented inside those terrible chins

Ships crossed the cracks on their faces
They gathered wool on their fingertips
Sweet fires were damned
With the ivy with the pus of flowers
The hyena the chameleon the turtle sang
And in blood-stained flight
He grew corals inside his esophagus

Rose instead of avalanche
Tonsured breath
Sleeping light
Obelisks folded by terrible winds
Bonfires that rise above the lip
Over the daily drinks
Of the poor with gaping mouths

Everyone clamored inside their magical clothes
The trees polished their leaves
King for flower
Next to the beloved seers
Who grew beetles
Around their breasts

Dead women spat out by perverted dreams
The leaven deep within their eyes
Cut the opium cut the tarantula of our good friends
Flowering inward more frightfully
Than the night itself

Chlorophyll on his fingers on his skin
The sounds were ripped out
A bitter fog
And the loaded dice of the gulfs of Europe

They were touching his marvelous temples
Soft neighing could make the eyes grow
Through sweet poisons
He abandoned the word inside Hell's mouth

It was then that the ghost began to grow larger
Between sobs and smiles
Storms were unleashed over sandy hair
And the fire inside his mouth lit the cursing
Like the great fish in his soul

This is how they cursed the city of lovely forgettings
That bitter city of dark memories
The flowers speak the turtles speak
Laughter reigns in bubbling flames

King for one final night
And the eye split open over the shared grave
Roots divided like beautiful faces

The eyelid fell in fragments
Pure waters opened his chest
The skulls were covered in alcohol tongues

King for one last night
The vampire's flower
The slow sparrow hawks of his shadow
Mad for oblivion for cruelty

His dreams petrified forever
Blood, ash, memory's celestial eye
And the WORD was burnt in the invisible kingdom
By its HERMETIC
Image

(1940)

VERTIGO OF THE NIGHT

I follow the flame through the abyss
After warming my hands in the past
I am and I belong to silence
To black hate
With its motionless horror
I am the target that the birds peck at.

Maybe into the dense darkness
Where longing
Knits the banderoles children spit out
The brides greet each other
While I remain silent and remember
This love
This amusing love
The only love that could save me from the waves of memory
"You will be tall and you will reach great heights"
I remember: this is nostalgia.

One follows the trail of a space
Two times more oppressive than my heart's emptiness
I will die for emptiness
Not like one who always trembles at the edge of the abyss
But like the damned man
Who faces imagination and for the first time sees his own face .

This is why I allow my heart to descend into memory
To remain inside silence
So that I will always be
That pure movement of dream.

(1945)

ALICE IN WONDERLAND

When the tree gives free reign to its desires
When the tree sees with its eyes wide open and recovers its sense
    of smell
And notices us we who identify with the lake's weariness
Despite the anger of clouds and hands begging for mercy:
It is then that the imagination is shaken by inevitable cataclysms.

Someday the knot that perturbs memory's thread will come undone
Someday there will be no difference between dream and wakefulness
And you, beautiful stranger, you will will be free to lie down on
    pleasure's grasses
Mistletoe and hawthorn will grow on your chest
Your gaze will be my gaze
And every afternoon you will sit and wait for me at the entrance of
    the very gulfs you now hurl me into
Those black gulfs feared by dogs
Wrested from the territories of the devil.

We will not have to concern ourselves with
Attacks without risk-taking
We will not have the cloud for you to benefit from
Nor the stone made to harden our eyes and noses
We will not have me feeling sorry for my poor self.

Man will go back to being a plant
A creeping nose
A wandering bird
In good terms with its five independent senses
Surrendered to a cruel and flawless disorder.

(1948)

NATURAL ENCOUNTERS

Once the blindfold is removed
We find ourselves in the same room we visited before
The sun holds surprises for us sometimes
And without knowing why we now discover
The ghosts that disturb our tongues
The mind's shape itself.

Who could have imagined that in
A place like this one, crossed by the light
I should find myself and my lover transformed into automatons
Visiting the sick
Looking to the right to the left to the sky.

My beautiful beloved is generous despite my pride
Despite the clouds that consume our souls
Despite the waves lashing at the shutters.

I beg you, do not spread the secret
Do not disclose my adventures with alchemy
Look childhood friends forever my friends
Behold my marriage to a ghost.

(1948)

THE GHOST OF RENE MAGRITTE

When he discovered the glowworm's ineffable trace
Strange beings began to surround him beings one normally associates
    with fury
Beings at whose step sound becomes silent
Who invite you to the bottom of the sea to the bottom of the sky
To a storm of objects.

And you René Magritte you walked dragging your ghost along
With your unknown world tempered on the forge of desire
On the ring of our imagination
You wore a ghost's finger on your finger.

You saw yourself in the angel
Whose bolt of lightning was the merciless tree
You recognized yourself in the tree
Whose glance was a perfect statue of flesh and blood
You became the window's torture before the infinite.

Gale fire that travels from head to toe
Fire to cry by and fire to laugh with
Fire next to which you are you with your eye of fire
Nostalgic fire.

So much useless life
So many mirrors sacrificed to the will of the magic circle
So much heart at the edge of the abyss
Why should life – the life we often remember – be useless?
You know why René Magritte
You know from the lightning and you know from your love
You know through the most perverse of clouds.

You walk and unwalk the road that is no longer the same road
Familiar and unfamiliar objects enter your room
You invite them to dinner
You speak and you let them speak
You offer them alcohol you are as enigmatic as they are.

I turned to myself
Trembling before the page on which I write you
With my coat forgotten with indifference I say to you:
Enter ghost of flesh and blood
Enter.

(1948)

GOOD SENSE

A mirror always separates the familiar from the unknowable
Its matter wraps bodies in a magic substance
It feels their pulse and knots their hands
Reduces them to dismal slavery.

The mirror makes itself edible now
Man feels the desire to accomplish great deeds by eating the light
But the objects get up
They get ready to resist the attack.

Magic persists
An entire reality unexpectedly transmutes itself
While feeling and logic become absurd
The eye is right
And I continue to separate myself from my own image
I submit myself to the law of compensations
I engage in lively conversation with objects.

This is essential:
To bring destiny into the world
To furnish the mirror with wings
To feed from the resistance of objects
To heed neither gravity nor what leaps out of mirror
That *mon cher ami* is *le bons sens*

(1948)

THE SLOTHFUL ONES

I

They are warm turbid and vicious
Followed in clouds on lips in insomnia
Panting cruel voices
A story for impenetrable branches
Like an insensitive sea of hallucinations

They are warm during the afternoon
Breath surrounds the breast
Which looks like a new story
As well as the eyelid which hardens
I am the sea the sky exposed to perversions
To solitude to fog: protuberant thigh
In short, a swan watching its own descent
Which I adore.

II

Now they are spitting out their hands
The rotating tree around their breasts
The voice swarming
Thighs gathered up
Thick waters shake
The carotids.

Their desires descend they rise to their foreheads
A spider shaking in the air
Which is their instinct
They are born again pure forgotten and abrupt
With persistent faces
Movable faces, hollowed out sphincter
Their designs are black
For love they search each other out.

They are thirsty, the tooth leaps
Let us split the ghost
The sleeping eye adheres to their wombs
Later to their eyelashes
Well-pressed against the tree their torn clothes
They make themselves findable in dream.

III

Love is mine
Contracting the dark tongues of memory
Opting for light delta opening existence.
Eat laugh strangle yourself
Start by backing up in front of the mirror
Love each other without respite
Freedom.

I held transgressable lights opening my lips
I was wall
Desirable bridge
Nevertheless loosened limbs passed before the light
Hostile disgusted they laughed
Eye to algae
Algae for arm
More desirable than stupor.

IV

Warm ones, troubled and vicious
Poisonous adorable ones
Adulterous choleric kidnapped
Women, you are there in your waste inside your souls
I love you
You etch your fingerprints on flesh
You raise your cheekbones your wrinkles your belly
Go on, fall down, move your tongues

I love you I fall I see myself falling
I bridge I wall I solitude
I in the adorable castle
Save me.

(1940)

Braulio Arenas
Chile
1913-1988

THE ENIGMA'S WORD

I

On the wall in the mirror
In the hair that knots the night
In the mirror
In the tortuous passage from bird to oil
On the wall
On a balcony for each light
For every shadow for all company
Made to the measure of the two of us

You walk from cloud to cloud as if you were the rain
From enigma to enigma as if you were the only answer
You walk among glances as if you were a tear

You can't wait to see yourself as soul over the earth
For a nation of birds to appear under the ocean (the cloud will be left
    exposed to the elements)
You are still looking for the time you lost to ecstasy
When you rubbed your ring and guessed the time
For love

II

I defined the word *soul* in accordance with your lips
I waited for the night because you were visible only in the dark
And again for a while at dawn and again and again
Sometimes for just a few seconds
And it felt like a party when you stayed the entire afternoon
Now I make out your eyes through the memory of you

For a few seconds
How can
A few seconds

Account for a lifetime

Yet those moments
Have corrected centuries of my existence
They have perfected me when I could no longer wait to kiss you
The hours did not pass while I thought of you
They began beating when you approached

So different one hour from the another
Hour of the heart the lip's hour my soul's hour
The bird's hour
Like an oil stain over the ocean

III

The plaster was trying to get its share of that joyous afternoon
    Certain stalactites behind the dark bars of a cage were singing the
eternal scream of the fireplace
    Three young women went by pressing a bunch of flowers to their
chests*
    I was about to leave with just a few minutes left before my depar-
ture.
    It was impossible to be overjoyed.
    I had a premonition that the morning would be luminous
and clear
    Could the three young women be of significance in my life?
    – Bah– , I said without thinking.
    But after losing sight of them I began to wonder: why had I stated
with such conviction that they were pressing a bunch of flowers to
their chests?
    – Bah– , I said once again and immediately thought about those
mysteries one never quite manages to put a name to and which seem
to hover in the air like bees around the bouquets which young women
press against their chests in the early morning hours.

* Their names are Acha, Fatima, Mariel.

IV

The cliff is an apterous insect
The mist carries you without missing a wave
The mist makes the most of the last strands of light
And puts the last touches on its radiant tapestry

You are rehearsing your challenge on that tapestry
You insist on attracting the raft
You persist in being both cliff and shipwreck
Life anoints your lips with waves

Go back to summer to your last summer
The women and their boiled eyes * are walking across the courtyard
From so much traveling down the road of life only love can trace
The road of dream which this poem travels until it belongs to you

The sun and the moon brought their eyes to a boil
Their glances take care of the rest
Their glances are finishing the drawing
Of this moving tapestry which depicts life
A ship crosses the horizon
Slowly
Slowly like pain forming inside a tear

V

For a better destiny
And the aroma of coffee which greets the traveler in the morning
Where the little black bull crosses the prairie
This morning I knew only about throwing projects out
Like pulling a thread through a fire

The prairie folded at the corners and suddenly hurled itself
    against the train
Stars cups of coffee little bulls and all

*I am reminded of the eyes of the ''Lady of Elche''

They were humming an old song
"How can the past"
Yes the past that is no longer a project
A tortuous past that "became a cricket and waited until dawn"
Yes, until dawn and all through the night without skipping an hour
And the cricket repeatedly sang out the time
Inexorably like cream in a cold cup of coffee

And another hour will have devoured its seconds
I can't wait to kiss you at that hour
Time will never wrinkle the hour's pure face
It is the face of the hour liberated in space
Mirror of your love: I can't wait for the hour when I will see myself
    in you

VI

Mouth over time
Words licked by fire
And the night is dream's grass
Like an unnecessary sea
For an indispensable shipwrecked man

Sky without railings
Without abyss without eyes
Led by the hand of
Of love

The rain is pouring down
Glass turns into night and fools the windows
The jungle turns into a bird and fools the sky
Love turns into bread crumbs to attract the sparrows
Man turns into dream. Woman turns into eyelid

Why go on?
Let's continue
Let's keep going until the poem devours its own words
And all that is left is a blank piece of paper

We will gladly exchange
For a stanza of alexandrines
Or a sip of fire water

VII

Not a single glance is left of that eye which ten generations of
cyclops cried over. The eyes of the young female bicyclops spoke to
her dreams about those twenty years. Reality's pillow is standing on
the other side of an avenue lined with eucalyptus trees and is mimick-
ing the birds wearing white corsets. The young tricyclops merrily put
on the corsets which are still beating, warm corsets, corsets which
wear their nervousness like feathers.

Corsets and hair were all that the night allowed the young cyclops
to see, seeing that he was blind for life. But cyclops are blind nowa-
days, just as roses don't sing like they used to. There was a time when
roses sang and children cried. Not like today. They see with eyes that
are wide open because of hunger. There was a time when fishes
chewed tobacco and spat, a time when all the houses in the city had
roofs made of gold so that chirping swallows could come to rest on
them.

The blind cyclops allowed his hearing to guide him and was thus
able to tell his native island apart from other islands. Now he can only
make out the phosphorescent corsets that slip down this bitter night.
Some of those corsets as well as the women's hair are gathered in the
street. Beautiful women who fly and are happy. He goes up to them,
but listens as they erase themselves all of a sudden. He again places
his pillow on the ground and dreams about them, but his dream has
changed. A burning diamond is stuck to the eye on his forehead and
he shouts and wakes up, because there was a time when love was
everything, a time when the sun was just a mirage visible from far
away and not from up close.

VIII

Good-bye, good-bye word of the enigma
You have arrived.

The words have kept their word
Lips have accomplished their kisses
Eyelids accomplished their dreams

On the wall in the mirror
In the hair
In the calming murmur of the tree the birds fly
The mirror reflects the balcony where love knots the couple's
    neighborhood
To shed light on the enigma

Enigma of love which is always an enigma that sheds light
Creates a sky at the expense of the earth
Oh unnecessary day
For an indispensable night

Oh lucid coal
I can't wait
for the diamond hour.

LOVE

Not one of my thoughts can come about without the clarity of your reality. Not one of my thoughts can exist without the purity of your dream. There is not one of my thoughts which wasn't rendered transparent like a diamond by your love.

The moment I met you, you surrendered your forehead intact to my delirium so that these torn images could alight on it . Without you I would know nothing about the world. You reveal the storm to me and your body becomes transparent so that I may enter your love and devour its fruit.

In order to see you I have closed all the doors, I have cut off all the threads, every bridge, every exit. I want to come face to face with you. Always, from the moment I met you, I have been alone with you. Not one hour of the day or the night have I spent alone without you. Neither in dreams nor awake have I ceased to be with you, always.

This, for better or for worse, is what I understand as love.

TO THE HALLUCINATING BEAUTIES

They named gold,
the panther, the hoarfrost.
They blow with force
on any road.
Behind their love
ravings are fixed
the seagull rolls over
with anticipated sea

They smile as they ask
for forgetting and demand
mercy for their deeds,
sometimes furiously
They request death at will
with plenty of luxury,
exhausted, motionless,
birds from a golden age.

A tide of lamps
creeps up to their shoulders.
They are frantic when left alone
punished by life.
They display their dreams,
they copy them down with their fingernails
and walk raising
a glass of water to their ears.

They sit before
an auditor of shadows.
They distill beauty.
They speak forcefully.
They reduce dream to sun,
thirst to sphinxes.
And life feigns
its own piles of blood.

A beam of light proclaims your dreams,
Yolanda, while other
lights chain them down
reduce them slice them.
Your associated eyes
come down to drink
the lunatic asylum
of your mink breasts.

Delirious stars
like bread crumbs
expand in the middle
of your blood stream.
All the swamps
with mystagogic fevers
make tombs sprout
before the flood.

Their hair seduces
a soft whiteness like nit.
Inspired, they raise their eyes
drown themselves
and some give out kisses
like beautiful scars
and complain earnestly.
Unearthed bodies.

In their scarlet corsets
they keep sweets,
feathers, matchboxes.
Hysteria is invincible.
The dragon is not ash
and the pillow is not the dream:
abstract eyes are
watching the sea grow.

They are fifty
miles tall
and wear wheat feet

with sickles in their shoes.
They burn on genuine beds,
sleepless and asleep,
on hairy islands
born with cruelty.

But nothing,
onomatopoetic straitjacket,
nothing moves more
than these fixed ideas.
Search furiously,
go through the sieve
torn to shreds: death.
They live for delirium's sake.

Mad breathless bee-queens,
the air is being trimmed.
Pale one put to death,
hurt by a whisper,
she follows more attentively
than a wise man the shocks
that strike not her, but our miserly reality .

THE OBVIOUS SIGHT

A clearly interior woman
I saw her in her eyes
I hugged her around herself and kissed her on her lips
As far as her feet were concerned I took off her shoes
As far as my life is concerned she answers to it
As far as rightness was concerned the two of us were right
We possessed dream
We possessed pleasure and the value of its answer
For life
I will hold your youth in my arms for life

A fisherman was mending his nets in your eyes
Such a beautiful afternoon I am tearing my forehead apart
    for dream
I am shaking off all notion of slavery with the help of my hands
All notion of reality which now lays claim to dream

That afternoon
All the afternoons will be saying that afternoon
All of love's kisses will be repeated in that kiss
Latent love made manifest in life

Little hand among all hands destined to serve as light for my destiny
Little dream you go from here to there like lightning rides the
    eye of the storm
Little dream you take this little hand by the hand
The entire sun was not beyond the cherry for these lips
Therefore the swordsmen forests buried their scythes
In honor of Saint Pol Roux's daughter whose name is Divine
Because even though so little time has lapsed a furious
    legend has enriched the sea
This solid sea
Without exit

EVERYTHING IS POSSIBLE
WHEN LIFE IS IMPOSSIBLE

I

By the middle of the week we'll call it *w*
Deafening quarry but also gnome
The gloves he wore on his ears
Spoke to him in hushed tones about emotional good-byes

Years ago those gloves belonged to a beekeeper
The other half of the week is already forgotten
The gnomes are sun-tanning lazily
And hang from the palisades
They think of nothing as they stare at the stonecutter
And shake their gloves like a *w*

II

The sky was sown with swallows
A little hole allowed the moon to revolve around itself
It came back as the moon every summer
But the mountain kept holding on to an Inca temple
And moon beams fell on abandoned treasures

When they least expected it on that day long awaited
They exchanged most expected jungles for the least expected jungles.
After fluttering in the rain the leaves
Could not go back to their trees and remained suspended in the air
    in silence

I remained silent before life. The days went by,
One after another the days went by like train cars
Sometimes we would arrive at a resort and immediately fall asleep
I must add that I never fell asleep without first watching a young

Woman comb her hair in the room across the hall.
The hotel lay silent like a dead soldier
The young woman's hair unfurled through the open window
She strangled my dream until I cried.
On other occasions we came to a eucalyptus forest
And the same young woman (or another woman) took it upon herself
    to set the tablecloth
On the ground which was covered with leaves that smelled of
    summer rain
And I could not stop expecting that long expected day
I could not stop waiting for that long awaited day
When I would recover my speech

III

But the days kept going by one after the other
The days went by and my heart was closing up like a fist
I took part in a day-long hunt
It seems that there was a monster terrorizing the entire region
And when night came I got lost in the mountains
And ended up in front of a cabin which glowed
And there I met the huntress dressed for supper
She was expecting me since the least expected day
Until the long awaited day came
The days kept going by

Oh swallow please come back
The threatening sky is frowning
You resemble a mask and this is a splendid costume ball
The women are dressed in perfume
They raise their chins and turn up their noses
While their eyes smile
They keep their warm hands inside mine which are cold like ghosts
And no matter how many days go by
Compassionately they invade me with their perfume

Do I come from nothingness?

Why do I so wish to hold on to your body and run endlessly through
    love searching
Searching for what search?
On the least expected day and without expectation the night is looking
    for a day to cry on
That least expected day finally meets its own welcome
And we walk down a welcoming road
A road made from your kisses
For you woman I have always remained the same
No matter how hard I try to convince everyone that I come from
    nothingness

IV

They say that the sea is unforgiving
They say that it never forgets
The sea gave the better part of its life to the tide and held it
    tight in its fist
The sea's heart was like sealing wax
Life had decided to close the music hall half way through the season

Lime pyramids and an eternal passerby
The coast's reflection was like a sleepless window
The doves I let loose in another poem appear here again
And they perch themselves on top of the lime pyramids
Good-bye good-bye I walked across the abandoned music hall
A woman's glove is all that is left behind on the table
I leaned my elbows on the table and looked out through the sleepless
    window into the sea
This is where this endless poem ends

THE COURTYARD

The courtyard is strewn with cookie-cans. A courtyard without windows, without doors whose walls are covered in glass. In this courtyard the women are wearing white aprons while they suntan.

Outside a bus whirs by. The day is calm.

But, who has so misinformed me?

There are doors, so many doors. And windows. The women have finished cleaning the last tin cans from the courtyard and are now shaking the orange trees which are heavy with ants. Children are pouring through doors and windows as though they were coming home from a nearby school. The women greet them with gleaming faces.

The sound of the bus is heard again. The afternoon is drawing to a close.

But, who has so misinformed me?

The women are dead, definitely, distantly dead. Their sons have grown up and could easily be mistaken for any one of us.

THE ENCHANTMENT

She stared into the sea for a long time.

She then turned her back to it and started walking home.

Seemingly disdainful.

Standing on the shore, however, her open hand had left a trail of salt, as if sowing, as if working.

The thread of salt went from the water's edge to the very threshold of her mansion.

And not once did she turn around to see if the ocean was following her.

She was perfectly aware that the ocean had licked the salt and had fallen into her net like an African pygmy.

THE CAT

The cat had built a pyramid of chairs on the bed. Perched on top like a circus acrobat, the weight of his body caused the building to sway.

The test consisted in getting as close as possible, dangerously close, to the pillow where lay a bunch of carnations. The cat inhaled the smell wisely, in a to and fro of madness, of screams, of dreams with pointed roofs, which anyway, represented the concept of the African jungle.

Jorge Cáceres
Chile
1923-1949

THERE IS A GREAT DESERT

There is a great desert between Madame and me
A lion's head cast in plaster
It resembles one of the objects I have just built
An object much like the current summer
The lion's jaws are two corncobs from the most recent harvest
Which have been dragged around the entire countryside
Its eyes are two dried-out lobsters
Its back is represented by an immense granary where English
    tourists often get lost
They will be coming from the seashore
Toward the opposite side of Guyana
The first tourist often visits me at six o'clock
He usually leans both his elbows on a table laden with delicious
    sweets
When he brings a bread basket brimming with bits of lamb-meat
    from the kitchen
The guests in formal dress disappear under the resort street lights
They carry their food in their pockets
His attitude has changed in the last few days
This change is due
To the fact that he works eight hours a day on the construction of a
    pyramid of water sprinklers
Under which he his wife and their six children will spend the summer
A great number of white rats are running in circles around his nose
He nails them to a board at the entrance to his hut
With great eloquence

(1938-1949)

JUSTINE

On July 8th, 1787, a woman crossed the very spot where the
    Henry IV bridge stands today
Overwhelmed by the weight of a thought she bent over the well
And with a gesture like a gust of wind all the eyelids in the world
    were shut
Like phosphorous windows which turn black with the morning light
In the depth of the forest the light falls in the form of ash
And mysteriously through the branches a woman's stocking
    is the Holy Bible
Wandering under the Paris storm
Surprised by an eye fixed on its prey
A woman walks on snow stained with ermines
Not far from the castle which she will enter
Inversely to the black line that runs across her breast
But lightning stops her dead in her tracks and in the forest
The trees let out their last signals and expire
A window opens into mist like a gun shot
A woman dressed in white comes in
She is wearing felt earrings
Her phosphorous hair is too fresh
She stops for an instant in the middle of the dragon-sun made of
    artificial light which seems to grow out of balconies hoisted by
    pillars of haze dissipating into the arch of her lips of
    burnt-gunpowder
She takes a bad turn
Her breasts discover the shortest route
To the top of the chestnut trees
As in the old books for children
Where we suddenly discover that the consonants cancel out the vowels
Then on each and every Viennese window a lamp evaporates
And in the intense atmosphere the lava-lightning of earthly
    paradise slips away hurling darts around which simulate
    the fascinating fringe of scriptures written in invisible ink
Lightning is the fairy's cousin on the telegraph wires
If I say Bressac it is to provide the reader with a clearer understanding
Of this game of hands his slave is the perverse lightning-rod

Which has now and forever collapsed into the beautiful passenger's
    bouquet
Which is circling a lamp of firecrackers a white-hued solution
    of sorts
Purple-tinted filaments of polar stars used for dunking
The day's scents locked themselves into the observatory
Where two canaries discovered vitriol candies
A momentary flower on the windowsill
The black sitting room of dream-applied photography
She knows that my thoughts spin
Like a throbbing needle on the sphere
Night falls with the batting of an eyelid
Night opens its chastity belt of ibis feathers
A woman naked but for a yellow-striped chastity belt which
    can issue the storm's double resolution is walking on the
    edge of a city whose name is "I don't know"
Under her glove of snake tracks of water spurts of a garden of
    poisoned darts
A head passes by – Monsieur Bressac is meeting me for tea –
A rendez-vous of the poorest kind on the snow overlooking
    the reindeer
Before the abyss of vague limits
A head with a doll's double tongue that says yes and no and never
Falls dead rolls over the enchanted floor twice as purple
And a masked bird crosses the width of the eaves
Carefully threads the invisible cone with red string
Needle and straw in a forest carpeted with light
The day's pleasure is an arrow dressed in night's black skin of
    incandescent steam
Brewing up a storm in a champagne glass
Justine
For an instant a lightning bolt remains suspended on her finger
Like an aquamarine in a black beach
Sewn to the inside of her eyelashes a window of air currents

(1938-1949)

THE CAPILLARY SYSTEM

The capillary system of the woman I love
The one who crosses the beaches without dreaming
The only one who can breathe the salty airs
When her way of laughing with pride
Can no longer be contained in the sky.

The capillary system of the woman I love
Is the miserly birds for me
The fire-winged birds
That die from laughing
Birds that clutch my eyes
Over the weighing scales of furtive feathers.

They are unaware of the burning crowns
Ermine crowns that resemble you move no longer
They fear the air of the edged seashore
And the starfish
Always daily.

(1938-1949)

PAUL KLEE

Be an accomplice of the landscape beating in full flight
Like a well-fed fire hands up!
The children are guilty of their endless green eyes
They have dispelled the sky in broad daylight
With charming smiles
With games that are no longer innocent
The clouds in the bathtub the respect for our parents
And the great traps of precise calculations.

The beaches are being watched by bargain blind men
The sense of touch in the swimmers' eyes
And fever's curve over the great rocks
They have wasted their time on the seashore
Without a word of compensation they remain at their posts
Over the delicious scales of good weather

The octopus the wolf the tapir the ermine
Are just memory's game
Enhanced by the animal scale
A face in the desert and the hand in the middle of the landscape
Have broken the ring of eulogies.

(1938-1949)

IN THE BEAR'S NET

To Max Ernst

The storm cuts the threads that link the trees
A girl plays riddles on snow which flaunts the colors of
    a pheasant's wing
It is here that a black wind enters the forest like a gloved hand
Without this implying to the woodcutter that his three children are
    wearing wild hazelnut earrings
The cynical gesture of a woman wearing a crown hovers over the
    chimneys
The woman is preceded by the recent flight of three geese
    of invisible colors
She comes in she goes out of her moon balcony
Wearing a mask of feathers that spin toward the horizon and
    slip into the tropics
By strange coincidence her stockings are two mirrors set against a
    white ivy background
In her throat sleeps the coral snake that will drag her to the bottom
    of the ocean this afternoon
And her wristwatch is spinning very fast like a blind man
    who has misplaced his cane
But real as ever the image of the woman at her window appears again
Although this time her hair is a propeller moving in the
    direction of fire-flies darting about at dusk
With a smile. There is a nicotine stain on her forehead
This is why the birds fly backwards
Great birds for passengers
And inside the magnetized porcelain of spark-plugs
The lightning bolt decides how to best light up lakes for children

In the meantime a man with a sparrow hawk's head has just gone
    out the back of the house
With his jacket flung over his back and a mask that changes colors
according to the pressure of steam
Tulip color gas color ginger color Degas color araucaria trees' color
But an air of seriousness hangs over the lamps in that house

And the nightingale falls dead under the weight of its feathers
As does the tree under the weight of a thousand dying nightingales.

Stepping lightly like a hare the hunter comes out of the forest
His enchanted cartridges give shape to the Milky Way
While the light from freshly scraped fish scales
Blinds the businessmen traveling West
Like some system of lightning-rods a man wearing reindeer skin
    gloves suddenly appears
He points his revolver at the author's heart
But three somnambulist girls are walking on the snow
Carrying three bassoon-colored stars on their heads
And three magnetized suns.

(1938-1949)

THE WONDERS OF THE EARTH AT AN ALTITUDE OF THIRTY METERS. THE WONDERS OF THE SEA THIRTY METERS BELOW

The orchid wearing its underwater camouflage once again bursts into
    the golden frame of the chiffonniers of night
Of day but in sparkles of vampires that come out of a scarlet-
    lacquered forest in the form of blue flames
Great flames that turn into mummies inside the storm's threads
Great flames that are nothing but the definitive conjunction of
    luminous coconut trees opening and closing at the whim of
    misty window-panes
Flames of sinister perfumes dressed in goose feathers
Which stand out because they form a ring made of shellac
A crown of rock salt but when the country hour strikes
The one thousand birds that pierce the rock crystal can fit into
    a beam of light
Without bearing in mind that all those apartments which provide daily
    and nightly comfort remain hanging in the air by themselves
But they sunk the furniture into boiling waters
Good and evil disperse and remain confined to jars whose personality
    is barely symbolic of old India ink
Even though the word India is written over the invisible objects
    of the world's darkest episodes
This afternoon I am walking among planted trees that betray a large
    diluted nicotine stain on the back of a swan
Swimming inside a glass disappearing briefly into a transparent room
Where four Venetian glass heads of four burnt-sugar statues of
Mozart have been laid to rest
In the sky a raging storm of champagne
Wears a black fringe of ermine waterfalls or a lioness caught by
    surprise in the middle of a dream
And on the worn railings of the gamekeeper's house stains show up
    that can determine the age of evergreens
While reassuring the man that the woman he loves will reappear on
    his night table
Man and his business
In this case the woman is wearing a beaver's muzzle

And in order to protect her nakedness she walks quietly over
    a bed that opens into a greenhouse of very white plants and
    very black furniture
By sheer coincidence the man is wearing a black and white mask like
    the multicolored filaments visible inside Wifredo Lam's liana
    lamps
The forest opens with a blast
And in the city time has come to milk the cows
While pearls are raining down in the stables
And this is why the air is a blond woman
In the aimless convulsion of Spanish balconies a jade hand is
    feeding a jade canary
At the bottom of the well magnetized eyes reveal an organized system
    of transparencies
They have already called each other three times today
As if the gagged woman at the window were not unfurling her hair
    in the direction of the South Pole.

(1938-1949)

NEVER

To Jacques Hérold

From behind the curtain the clown waits for the roulette to go around
    one last time: it will come up white
White this time and always but black in defiance of chance's
    golden nacre
A tapestry of frozen light issued from a certain glance
Escaping the one thousand pipes that dissolve when one faces South
When facing North man will witness the explosion of his cuirass
    bouquet of radiolarians
The landscape turns to glass as it takes on the shape of an egg
A hexagonal fan for the destruction of love
A formal plan for those who abuse a woman's glance every time
    she turns into antennae
When she shakes her hand a glove conceals a mummy odor
And a wave of turquoise steam rises like a ball of small Milky
    Ways that feed
As they make their way down a naked woman comes out to feed
    the birds
Oblivious to fire the dragon discovers a spring of sorts between her
    breasts born nowhere but guaranteeing its return by leaving a trail
    of fresh bread crumbs
Pure water dragon for you to watch its passing
Pain and pleasure come out of the egg
They promise you a bunch of mental butterflies with their grins
And the distance between the forest and the bed is the winter snow
    on your double ermine sex
Assuming the attitude of shots which go straight to the heart
And shine when the third light is turned off
Only when you take into account that the fringes on the light excite
    the imagination of the dragon-fly coming out of the basement
She has been knitting a net of lights around the children for one
    thousand years
Go down with the third light and the air will lock itself into preserve
    cans
Inciting the elves of putrefaction by means of stills that help

quicken man's breathing
An animal's breathing is no different
Someday the reproductive process will be yellow
A new sex endowed with one thousand petals under the care of the
Virgin
Someday the tiger's scarlet copulation
Under the perpetual vigil of the mole you will be fine
You will sleep soundly on the machine gun bed made from diluted
    topaz
Unless the child's ingenuity dictates otherwise.

Behold the little inhabitant of magnetized stone rises
When she waves her little wand one assumes that salt can turn
    itself upside down
Leaving behind a stain that can't be removed without the help of
    a mysterious liquor
The liquor we call Life turns into a lugubrious mask
And the tablecloth can no longer stand the bread
Nor the wine which takes on the shape of a revolving breast
Where a pearl can incubate with help from a woman's stocking
Trembling as it forms and at long last emerges from the guts
    of phosphorous
It rolls toward existence spurred on by the lark passing
    through rock-crystal
Maybe the mummified fish chases Vera around the house
Whispering in her ear that the boat has changed its course
A new rainbow pulls the landscape by the tail
A new rainbow of masked heads of moles made of white cilice
Draws the heavy drapes which boil under water
A new rainbow always
Never.

(1938-1949)

DOUANIER ROUSSEAU

To Aimé Césaire

The explosive midday sun hits at the herds of flame-throwers and
    sets the helpless throats on fire
Eyes of a helpless sun lightning-bolt under traps for squirrels
Under consecutive rains for lianas the palpitating flood-gates at the
    mercy of tattoos
Of boomerang hair the hands of mosquitoes
An ambushed breeze drags the crows' feathers
To the lion's entrance the upholstery roars
And the night will be brief around the fire.

Tribe without name.

In the great wells of pollen in the bamboo inside the felt
In treasures eaten away by voracious poppies
In the swaying reflections of the sycamore trees
In the chameleon's throat
On the back of a flood of eucalyptus trees thrice blackened

Tribe without name
On the trail of the wild pig
The surprise of chinchillas caught in a flash of light
In craters and the decay unfolding with the wind like the parrot's
    flight
A night of fine-smelling forests
Lightning plunges into white glass with red touches where the buffalo
    drink
One swig of the cayman's dream

Tribe without name
Full of the glances of comets at the end of the desert
Eagerly breathing self-love
For each breast that rouses there is a poisoned dart waiting
As well as a head dressed in python earrings
And totemic pearls

Which reach the last dimension in the panther's eye view
Without justice
Unfolding black fans made from vague pearls on an evaporating
  beach
Tribe without name
Without justice
To death

(1938-1949)

PAOLO UCELLO

Paolo Ucello you come out of the mercury well
Bartering the storm's roaring sounds in your carbonated heart
But some lost eyes wander on the black surface of a glass of vitriol
The thread you pull straight from the night is tangled on your
    forehead
You call at the door of the bird's heart you call it by its name
But I have seen you go around the world three times
Acclimatizing the quarry to an influx of turquoise
Acclimatizing your lips of wild opal to the ultramarine night
Ucello your undulating couch has just evaporated
And its eyelashes keep reminding me of your love for birds
Or your bleeding foot stepping over a bouquet of violets
On my pulverized heart in the white space left behind by that
    disappearing country scene
Over a breast of mineral water
Over a whole breast
Rising from a cushion like a tear
While an innocent glance slips by
One single glance Ucello
From a violet breast
Against a violet night

(1938-1949)

BEAR HUG

The woman from the country shuffles the cards plays solitaire
    incomprehensibly until the violet carbon is fully burned
This is what poetry becomes for me
As well as music and the other arts at the shot of a rifle
While inside the opaque room blue flyers begin to appear numbing
    the vague feelings of generations long gone
The gnome people are pulling the carriage of the night
And your eyes shine in the eclipse's puzzle
And a final flapping of wings comes out of the forest
And there is Braulio Arenas' house as designed by Yves Tanguy
On railings made of pollen which light up three lamps of ibis throats
    and flashes of bats flying at the bottom of the cave
Sheathing for beds with black fabrics and blue trimmings like a book
    spine
The black line which twists at the bottom of your eyes is taking on
the shape of a fan of incandescent filaments like a starfish
The black line the blue revolver and Kleist's ghost appears
    between us.
You turn your head back once but your eyes see the straight line
Over moss newly born on the windows
With the simple motion of the bouncing ball women use to seduce
    men
The balcony opens into the night with a defiant gesture
And two black arms take their place on the face of the clock
But on the beach the murmur of steps can be heard
And the impact of the forest ceases under the stars at the end of the
    enchantment
The balcony closes up in the footsteps of the dwarf
Hanging from the tip of a house that looks like it once was a hotel
    where quick decisions were made
In the middle of the XVIIIth Century
The damned arrow was cut
And love's arch will reach between two barrels colored with skill
The seer's crystal ball has exploded
And we enter the forest through the arrow
Without loosing one hair

(1938-1949)

Ludwig Zeller

Chile
1927

DOVE THAT WE DREAM

as the days pass over the water from high above
the shadows of the wings form spume and spray
flocks of birds return to invisible oceans
ships' wakes in the palm of my hand you listen
to birds migrating beating on the mirrors

I see the enigmatic ancient bird renewed
in the word that covers the surface of things with flame
your glance hard light reborn into the depths
tell me then singing your timeless leafiness
your secret plumage that has its dwelling with dreams
in impossible spaces and in tremulous petals
where the night makes its nest its eyes are
a black sky streaked with meteors

there it calls there hopes await the coming of rain
on parched mouth cut in the vertiginous face
so in some dwells the radiance of remorse
that I find in the inside of the eyelid

never may the spray return to silence

(1961)

Translated by Robin Skelton and Beatriz Zeller

LANDSCAPE FOR THE BLIND

I no longer remember when I withdrew from those wounds.
I go screaming through darkness, with my head I dig.
In the well the years multiply their swarm.
I don't know if I'm awake, if they give me milk or vinegar.

I open my fingertips into claws but they stretch
Beyond where the creaking voices throb.
She'll return with the rain; I have eaten my tongue.
Overturned, the globes settle their accounts.

Where are we groping – we seek a way
Beneath the sun, the stumps, the inscriptions of wrath.
We carry burning ices, we thrust hot coals
Into our eyes – sweetly our glances lick each other.

What do you see? I see you gasp like a fish in another air.
What do you see? Only a desert of mirrors and the knife.
What do you see? My root torn from the feathers of your bowels.
What do you see? I do not see. I only feel your presence.

(1964)

Translated by A.F. Moritz and Susana Wald

WHEN THE ANIMAL RISES FROM THE DEEP
THE HEAD EXPLODES

Today the ghosts are coming and across the table that swirls
I see the flowers spread over the parched crying
Of the eye that from the plate's center is watching
The jar of oil and its scorpion.

Suddenly the days closed, large leaves grew
Like skins of leopards lying in wait, they asked
My name in Aramaic, they broke the bottles
Of frozen lightning, those remnants of love polished by the sea.

Surely he is one too many, they said. The clock mismanaged
Its cogwheels and they turned those pulleys upside down
And among animals I wander – a warm-blooded being –
Along roadways I champ on my bit, loneliness.

Has the sun gone out? I ask. The children cry
And from all four corners I hear bubbles as they rise and burst
And lick without truce planks of wood, marinated edges
Of the Ark, under a canopy of fever follows the coal.

I do not want to see the guitar snap,
I do not want to see the pot overflow,
To see my claws, to ask again
If two and two make four, if the waters have truly boiled.

Where are we, dears? The sands of insomnia pile up,
Let us join the toys of terror, let us light the fuse
That it may part the moon in two halves and let us wait one
    thousand years...
                My squid
My mother in among the inks, suddenly starts her sobbing.

(1971-72)

Translated by John Robert Colombo and Susana Wald

VISIONS AND WOUNDS

It would serve us better not to hear the clamor
or to sew our eyelids shut in order to avoid
being blinded by vision, for man is only
smoking embers, a mirror bleeding at its root.

Lock after lock body to body
The days were etched they opened the darnel like lips
The hoary mantises leapt from one age
To the next great pillagers of death
Threshers listen to me here is the beyond

Blowing sand of rancor unbraids the walls
Where thousands of hands try to seize your flanks
Hinges made of feathers knife-edges beneath the skin
I see her asking about hoarse images tinkling of rings
When the opal encrusts its message in the flesh
Wounds that move wheatfields in the wind

I dream bottles full of salt violins
Their glass thinning the flames of that carriage of leaves
Lost in the myrrh-markets astray they drag you like sheep
Toward the nest of mirrors you remember with a sudden scream
    you turn
To live on your dreams giddy fruit in the tiger's teeth

Invocation that the waves repeat stirring skin planted
In the days light me the bonfire made of rancid bones
Laid on the anvil that sphinx of fever

With their nails the grapes of tremor the red-hot nipples
Clocks of pleasure raise beehives demand the impossible
Migration of the swarm toward the eternal present
Raising both legs to the blue flame
The razor I sought for a thousand years lost in your folds
Of lunar onion so I could stare at the precise geometrical curve
Of your breasts polished by the sea's din those tiny conch shells

Of hate-love love-hate dead schools of fish
On the beach where you pass by in a carriage of scales

I advance my voices my call is of one who plants his foot
In the depths of frozen seas on the transparent scab
The scaffold leaned against the unknown wall often closed
Waves suddenly petrified in the age of the knife

We slice the infinite body of light we hear
The bees humming they remind me of a hymn
Of eyes unearthed and covered with knots in the frying pan
Where year after year my life goes on burning in brine
Fierce creature idol sitting on its bowels
Dreaming and devouring our own offspring

On the endless waiting of remote eras I hear the rain fall
And the water is not illusion but tears shed there in the years
Where the chagual star grows the burning cineraria
The verse of a thousand veins cut and in the incision the Word
Resonant and now limitless that invades the land of the deaf
Where rust is gold with its darts where my life bellows
Beneath the fans of hatred the ivory branches
Sounding now rootless bloodless in the weariness of injustice
The massacre of the pure ones as warm as rice
Apportioned into anklets for her who is most beautiful into bowls
Of tears in the ochre stormy river of grief
Milky geography beating on the eyelid of the onion
As large as the heart that closed fist of torture

We hang skins on time in a parched desire for life
On a volcano's crest youth galloping bareback
On black eagles hurricanes bearing green burdens
Tell me what hands move those ropes far above
Stirring the nocturnal soup into which blood is raining
And in which I am only drifting timber
Beaten dragged to the pier the cretinizing
Labor that makes ink run the stain
That now no tide will wash away the incision in glass
Where the graphite hatches the mirages on the hide

Of woolly sheep the days of your love cross my life

Thread me on the wheel heralding a great pale sun
Spread open your legs that end in hooves
Ingeniously carved by adoring wanderers of fever
Those who polish your multicolored delirium with stones
When the ruby turns in the throat cut open
And throbs crackling trembling deafening itself
Until it is only the hollow center of silence

Domestic gods everyday gods ground
And boiled in the great black river inside the eye
And turned to dust by oblivion in some cave that blossoms
In leather thongs and strips of metal the fever
That reminds of the warm range of your arms
Up which I climb purple octopus of madness

Whirling burning memories to the root those heavy petals
That a new Crusoe raises in the summer of the impossible
Solitary beaches of insanity where he is always alone
Or visited by the bird of delirium that returns every hundred years
The violins that the tide drags ceremonial hiss
Of terror in the ribbons tied at the end of a bone
The use of murex among idolatrous peoples rehearsing
Repeating that song of rocking to and fro in the mechanical
And beast-like chair of torture they are merry until sorrow deaf
Like ice in the greatest desolation the dismantling
Of life the flame that is a name of the skin's other side
Where the mythic bird speaks in many tongues
From the moons of the mirror that I without lid or socket
Bleeding and wasting itself in its cage of apples

We imagine that we are not like gills out of water
Those plains where the brutal delirious frenzied rooster prevails
With its leather rattle pegged into its breastbone
Of gnawed silver and strangling it since that far-off time
As adverse and bittersweet as the taste of dried figs in villages
Where the blind see learning to sing
Raised on the tip of the word the eyeless sockets of Homer

On the points of the reeds dyeing blue his litany of questions
Asked as a way to drink the mythical image of the wind without
     understanding
Whether it is better to see or to sew the eyelids over the eyes
Soothed by terror only the flies hum above our wounds

The origin of all song is the dream flowering
In the occult that honey of somnambulist women
Clock with sex of bells tolling in the windstorm
Secret name etched beneath the bone of the palate
On cardboard funnels the chalk drags its rancid inscriptions
Spinning above a skull of transparent and real numbers
Those cups of storm throwing warm dice
On the rugged light of memory recollection of love

Come tell me about the seed of laughter you carry
Delirious toy made in the days a hope to arm us
Covered in ashes we hear the wound incurable mirage
Behind veils the bitterness on the pincers of all that exists

You rise above the car gearbox of vertebrae
As real as the passing of a shadow over the heart
Wings open in two in four in eight unfolded to the infinity
Of walls that open to terror and the cry – for what ?

Deliver me from your borders your angry edges
When I search like cattle at the end of the blind canyon
Animals driven through my dream searching for an exit
On the other side of light biting that rind of reality
Our food the acorn in the pig's snout
When I think of the Prodigal and I remember that old etching
With a tiny window opening toward childhood intact eternal
And then the father taking him in under the cape because he went
     beyond
All renunciation which is the act of remaining in this death
Where everything moves with the speed of our acts
And everyone pulls a thread from the concave mirror and listens

We are beating a dark drum and it was my heart
My old heart suddenly a thousand years old
Or ten thousand more than all its throbs
Like cranes leaping over the granary in flame
Witchcraft of your skin tormented tormentress
Idol of a thousand faces repeated multiplied
In the light of the diamond you fall and rise in perfect spheres
Of geometrical hymns that spread life
In millions of branches growing all around the fountain
A cavalcade of insects mounted on horseback in death
Or the horror beneath the iridescent hair of a raccoon denuding
The beautiful one of all her thorns under a cathedral wall
Made of ice quietude nostalgia for what is yet to come

We ask for other lights when close to us
Water runs until it makes our eyes close in tears
Life flows like ink our blood ebbs out to the sea
To the other side of God to the vinegar when you hear
The great bell tolling in this age of reptiles
Served at the table like claws in lemon sauce
Stirring slightly under the boiling light of opals

The last illusion is it within you rain which lights
That yeast of woman fragile as reality and like it
Only a sound of petals carried by the wind
To the other shore? Who is waiting for us there?

Are words only smoking embers?

(1976-77)

Translated by A.F. Moritz and Susana Wald

EAR-CLOCK

My father took a clock apart and its two halves spread
Across the white tablecloth – multiple wheels like ears cut
From that mechanical monster howling in secret as it crosses
The sphere where the face of minutes and hours laughs.
The diabolical parts were never pieced together again
And time ran freely there in my childhood.

                               Did the years go by?
I don't remember. Again and again when making a poem, linking
Word to word, image to image, once more I've torn apart
The black numerals that imprison the man living inside me
And I've dragged its parts to the sea, the pieces float, they sink,
Nothing but ball-bearings, splinters blown in the wind,
Papers that return and are nothingness, four corners of an empty
    earth.

At the bottom of the collage sometimes I hear my father laughing
Out loud, opaque millimetric time no longer exists and we can
Return to the kitchen table, hear my mother singing
Her melody of silence and see at the bottom of our pupils
The old miracle, the fleeting grace with which children look
At shining scissors when they cut clocks on the sand.

Who will free us from the blind bell? From the horrible
Mechanism in which I hear myself cry? The raving mare
Of mystery gallops out there in the dark. I hear birds hidden
In the branches of the pepper tree warbling. Eternity passed by.
    Never waking,
My bones whitened by cold, I am waiting for you here.

(1984)

Translated by A.F. Moritz and Beatriz Zeller

THE EYES OF DEATH

The days ache and the burning sand raises its fish scales
Over the eye in order to love in small boxes, quartz coffins
And forget the sores where the linden tree flowers year after year.
From this game I could separate those cuts
That yield coincidences, that fix the dates, could button up my wound
And be the deaf man who sometimes hears a distant murmur.

But death has double spectacles, eyes without lids
Like knives, when she advances shrouded in mysterious knots
And the pounding step of her dance sounds on the drum's parchment.
The marrow trembles, the sun tears itself apart; where is her image?
The table is set and on the white cloth those glasses broken
So long ago, so much glacial ice, mute ash.

We play, she and I: we pretend that in the tight weave of the rules
Bread is given to the blind who beg, that doors don't open
And the famous ovens are only a season of perfumes.
She plays the black pieces, I play the white, and days go by
Like centuries, her bishops plow the sea, they stir smoke high
    above and fall
Folded into corncobs my doubloons. On the knight's horse I jump
    back

And land in another time. Among a hundred faces covering me
I flee in search of that mask covered with inscriptions,
I dig into the scales of the immortal saurian that we all
Are in the embryo of origin, but my bones echo,
My skeleton creaks, the wind whistles, the skin of so much
Vain ardor is polished and once more naked I clutch the harpoon.

A mad lover like thousands before me, I jump into the ring
To dance bone to bone with the tyrant maiden death.
Dressed in black, she spins in the center. The music starts,
Passionately she beats the dust, we are wound one into the other,
The hook of her eyes burns all vain memory and all weariness
From lips that on lips are merely skin, are flame.

Come then, warm idol of so much sleeplessness, drink
From the root this marrow that wants eternity, make the drum
Spread my seed on the sands: I've waited centuries for you
My sweet eternal lover, I want your eyelids to cover me.
You open the door, languid, you smile. Tell me what you're waiting
    for?
I've finally arrived at your side, Lady of Silence.

(Toronto, January 17, 1984)

Translated by A.F. Moritz and Beatriz Zeller

THE INVISIBLE PRESENCE

To Frida and Laurens Vancrevel

To open the days like opening an eyelid,
Drop all the dead weight at last, leave (carefully
Turning on the lights), pass through walls as though they were
Doors, a vertical sea that closes into lips.

Without feathers, and now without hooks to sink into the flesh,
Skeleton of today, to slip away invisibly like someone opening the
     wind,
And whisper in the ear of the one who sleeps the syllables
That could wake him. The blue gramophone of memories.

To watch as the beautiful one rises out of torpor, eternal, unreachable,
And gestures, smiling at herself in the mirror.
To be able to move petals through the storm that is her head,
To pluck the strings when she asks herself the why of silence.

To be able to float on waters, turn in whirlwinds, be dust
In the desert where the strange caravan comes closer,
Bringing me the key, a warm nostalgia in each hieroglyph
When snow falls between hands and makes them translucent.

To know that someday we will be only a name in which you are
     burning,
Fleeting surfaces, beloved, invisible presence.

(1977)

Translated by A.F. Moritz and Beatriz Zeller

I. DREAM

I was in Paris at the gallery of Marcel Fleiss. I remembered then that a couple of months earlier he had sent me a catalogue with a reproduction of a painting by Freddie, "The Legionnaires of Pleasure." I had thought at the time that the picture was extremely small (23 x 23 cm), and yet I would have liked having it, despite the crudeness of color. Marcel, with his characteristic cordiality, invited me into the second room, on the other side of the courtyard, where I noticed that the painting measured three meters in height by three or four in width. Besides, it was completely different from the reproduction. A woman whose face I can't see because she's lying on her back has her legs spread open. The insides of the thighs seem immense to me, to the point of giving the illusion of a mountain. Men in camouflage advanced on her up a steep trail, trying by all means to forge forward toward her sex. Were they the legionnaires? I could see that they were armed with blowtorches like flamethrowers, laughing, their faces painted. I couldn't understand what they were saying, though I could hear the shouting.

Marcel Fleiss looked at the painting and explained that he did not smoke. I remembered the kitchen in my house in Toronto, where sitting at the head of the table I could see everyday a painting done by Susana in which a woman curled on herself lets us see an enormous nacreous thigh. The painting is called "The Origins of Fire" and depicts a friend of ours. In the dream I knew that that sex, warm as a petal, opened and closed as flowers do with the sunlight.

(At noon I was able to find Fleiss' catalogue. Not only is the painting different, but one feels oneself part of the breaking of a taboo different in each dreamer, and perhaps I too am one of those men trying to cross that sex.)

II. THE LEGIONNAIRES OF PLEASURE

To. W. Freddie

Bent over in a fold of the seething seas,
Fever's children consume themselves, with half
Their bodies set in walls to drink the sun
Under draperies where the thirsty ancient
And orthopedic deities are calling.

Reclining, they crowd together in elastic
Furniture where milk is falling down,
A waterfall within the eye of the wind.
Pierced, open, the weavers' shuttles flare,
Determined, pecking at hot ceramic thighs.

One after another dreams, each one advancing
Into his own labyrinth, unaware
That they are prisoners and but the piston
Of the senseless locomotive of sex,
As the glow worm goes through the darkness, coal
No more than smoke at the finish, like it or not,
There to remind us of another sirocco,
Sand crunching under the heaviness of night's rust.

They advance to open the well of feathers with blood,
That taboo, twice locked, which tormented the flesh of childhood,
The bread of mystery watched over in warmth and rent
By jaws the metal teeth sharpened, the pack of dogs
That will bring down the nacreous body on orgy's hinge.

Open today, the legs can at last tattoo
Those secret names with their bishops, can flay the skin
Of the walls and part the tentacles of that sex
Bearing them, avalanches, toward the tongue,
The flame-thrower's point, and there gaze under the drunken
Microscope at the root of the wounded mollusc
Roaring in the distance beyond their mothers

Who are sobbing now, burnt to the marrow,
Ash in the claws of the monstrous forbidden insect.

Memory spits its shrapnel against a wall of bones.

(1987)

Translated by Robin Skelton and Beatriz Zeller

THE GEARS OF ENCHANTMENT

The tear inside the eye rises and falls the surf
Combs there in the scream builds up in strata becomes our coach
An untied knot of hurricane your bed the bubbling foam the azure
Where a swirling wind pours itself into the four corners
Of a playing card whose face is nothing but crying I hear
A desperate scream from deep in the crevices of sapphire

The one we invited adjusts her tail for flight and we all
Work at untying the thread of a wing nut helix of the delirium
Of a horse that refuses to move and neighs stamping the ground
Scales leap down a shadowy pit cataracts of stones
And you smile in those cubes without doors the chivalric raging head
Slowly reshapes the torrent of vertebrae to a dice throw

Blood and semen, vinegar. On the bed we spin and hounds
Howl in the rigging of our sheets our dizzying thirst
Mockery breaks the light of the bee swarm flooding from the white
Into the black the eye leaps and is a die spotted by acid
I shout questions circling pounding on walls of ice
Deciphering names engraved by beings I have forgotten

The cards do not answer and life splits open brutal
Mirrors with the disdainful profile of a prince masked
As a falcon repeating versicles in a secret chamber
The tides are polished and the foam with pallid lips opens
The sinuous borders of a lank papyrus a dry withered storm
Grows still and in its rictus the sand bleeds and is silence

I try to interpret the night I cross the skin of your mirages
Enigmas that lay to sleep the image repeated yet unique
Of the square's fifth wall the invisible space behind your eye-rings
The space of my self-questioning when I see that others' ships are
    sailing
On the dream and then words and images flock to my throat
To be the name of Being and you cry out in the zero depth of the vault

Repeating that name I turn its syllables to solid quartz
While the jet of the beginning returns to being mere blackness
Plunging down through flayed strata and time's loud waves wash up
An empty shell it contains every axis symmetrical perfect
And memory shrieks in the rivers of lava the embryo of fire
Opens subterranean passages the mind creates a landscape that
     cannot be

I sit between lamps the light flakes off
In huge flowers roads pour out a rancid perfume
Of petals as soft as amber warmed by their desire
For the prayer wheels for the leaves of a wind of gemstone
And insanity from the moon which stops orbiting and goes down
Under water into my palms which are scars that emerged from
     within me

In an endless spiral light pumps blood and the broken
Breaths the glass fragments scatter the mystery
Like precious splinters of hurricane words are being broken
On flying edges of green obsidian and in its falling
The magic bough flashes in human eyes again to show the exact
Point on the illusory screen of drifting time

At the edge of my bed begins the stair whose every step
Is a different face like a bone enfleshed in night
We shout and into the salt we work our harpoons our words
Drunk and rutting explode into petals into claws and in us pulses
A thirst for the mental sun the skin of another light fire is poured
Into our vertebrae the milling wind whirls the rain's huge blades

The splinters of the wreck are inaudible the hawsers creak in their
     rings
There are waste spaces in the silence that covers you like eyelids
And you are no longer woman but a huge bird no longer bird
But the enchantment of windows that the sphinx once licked
Magic being fashioned from the mystery of quick crystal
Embryo that grows under the crackling of countless feathers

You are the skin of the live coal that shepherds drag
From season to season a conjuration adorning the secret body
Of night the oar of this fever creaks and splinters in the cold
In the pit of your breast you are hollowing a den the pall
Made of fragments described in pain the inverse language
When the wind changes and unfurls its silvers wings

My dark one my sweet one you are made of lips to drink your own
    thirst
In the straining cords in pleasure I hear your hanged body twist
Suspended in my bones a burning ember I hear you the deep
    grinding
Gears of wounds between ribs that bleed and flower
Time warbles and the almond trees are changed into melody
The only sorcery is your smile fragile woman conjuration of the ghost

(1986)

Translated by A.F. Moritz

BEATRIFYING THE
SYLLABLES OF THE GAME

To go down shouting to the bottom, to break the mirrors,
To tear out the cursed root as a dog would with its teeth,
To translate the bomb that flowers and explodes and bleeds,
To wait anxiously for the skeletons of jewelled marble
To come down the stairway, to seat themselves,
To cry, laughing, because all things are falsely similar
To the truth, mere simulacra of what we live.
To break our teeth a thousand times on words and complaints,
To parcel out the heart in verbs, articles, gerunds.
To fold ourselves into the pages of some book we love,
To fall asleep and dream prohibited delights and forget them,
To wake up at last and understand that the absolute rigor
Of death eating at us is only a bad copy of life,
Of what we lose in the dizzying game of love,
Of what transforms itself and is only a voice, an echo
Of the text haloed by a thousand tongues, the Spirit
Of Fire that, there in the garden, Eve spoke to Adam:

SDROW DNOYEB UOY EVOL I

(1992)

Translated by A.F. Moritz

SKETCHES OF INSANITY

Galloping toward the sea, crossing the sands at last,
To open the doors, biting my lips down to the frost.
Descending the spider's stairs, to hang from a thread
And blow the gleaming conch covered with spines.

To sail upstream along your forehead of white-shining Amazon
Questioning in her vigils the end of the wind in the sails.
If you could you would burn up all feathres with a breath.
Bent, your shoulders are warm cataracts, and the quartz beats.

Turn your ear-trumpet, your clock of curare toward me. Your story
Will always be the same since you always sharpen your loved one
Till you strike bone. Let's draw the splinter out of the dove,
Turn the days back, lay you on the drumhead and bleed you.

You break the needles, clockhands, spires, put a dromedary in a
        bottle,
Hide a jewel that rears up at the tightening of your thighs,
Admit you are a siren but hide your flame-stroked tail.
In the depths of your eyes green riders are coursing by.

Look at your palm. Can you hear? Only an echo of weeping,
Dizzying freshness of rain as it falls.
Become an urn: you want to drink all that is blue, all blueness,
Bit by bit, you repeat the intricate weave of a forgotten tongue.

(1992)

Translated by Theresa Moritz and A.F. Moritz

José María Arguedas
Peru
1911-1969

ODE TO THE JET PLANE

Grandfather, my grandfather! I am in the Upper World,
  above greater and lesser gods, the gods we know and the gods
  we do not know.
What is this? God is man, man is God.
Behold: the powerful rivers we love are cleaving the world
  like the fine threads of the spider web.
Man is God.

Where is the condor? Where is the eagle?
Invisible, like winged insects they lost their way in mid flight
  and are wanderers among unknown things.

God Our Father, God Our Son, God the Holy Spirit: I do not find
  you, you are not here any longer
I have come to the stadium that your priests and your elders call the
  World Above
I am in that world, comfortably seated on fire's back,
whitest red-hot iron, made by the hand of man, wind-fish.
Yes, they call it ''Jet.''
All the golden scales in all the seas and all the rivers could never shine
  like the jet shines.
The fearful knife-edge of sacred mountains shines so small down
  below: it has turned into a sorry icicle.

Man is god. I am man. Man made the peerless swallow-fish out of
  the wind.
We thank man, not man the son of God Our Father, but his maker.
Thank you, my father. No one knows what worlds your hurled arrows
  will reach,
Man-god make the swallow-fish move so that your blood may shine
  more at each hour.
Hell exists! Lord of lords, do not point the flying fire at
  the world for human flesh will burn.
May this golden swallow of the skies give life to other gods in your
  heart, each day.

Under the soft and infinite chest of the ''jet'' I feel more like earth,
   more like man, like a dove, closer to glory I feel.
My chest, my face, my hands turn into the sum of all the flowers of
   the world.
My sins, my stains evaporate and my body returns to sweet
   childhood.
Man, Lord, you created God in order to reach him. Why else?
You made him so you may touch him and yet you chase him away
   when he comes too close.
Careful with the knife-edge, the jet plane: it can penetrate deeper into
   you than earthly icicles can and will cut your eyes in half.
Too much fire. It is too powerful and free, this immense snow bird.
Careful, lest your son send you the heart-beats of death
The butterfly born of your hand can turn your head into ashes.
Man, hear me. Listen to me!
Under the jet-plane's chest my eyes become the eyes of that little eagle
   to whom I showed the world for the first time.
I am not afraid. My blood has almost reached the stars:
   the heavens are my blood.
Allow not the stars, not the celestial fish, not the god of rivers born of
   your eternal hands, allow them not to kill you.
God Our Father, God Our Son, God the Holy Spirit, Mountain Gods,
   Inkarri. God: my chest burns. You are me, I am you, in the
   untiring fury of the jet-plane.
Do not come down to this earth.
Continue your ascent, soar ever higher, reach the very confines of
   worlds that multiply eternally as they boil.
Mount them, glory-god, man-god.
You killed the God that bore you, the god that killed you, my brother,
   man.
You will not die now!

Behold! The jet-plane is circling above, urged on by the breathing of
   gods that were here from the beginning of time to the end of time,
   unseen, unknown.

José María Arguedas   *153*

TO OUR FATHER THE CREATOR, TUPAC AMARU

> *To Doña Cayetana, my Indian mother, who sheltered me with her tears and her tender ness when I was an orphaned child living in a strange and hostile, house. To the* comuneros, *in the four* ayllus *of Puquio who gave me strength and hope for the first time.*

Tupac Amaru, son of the Serpent-God. Made from the snow of the Salqantay, you are limitless and unceasing, your shadow enters this deep heart like the shadow of the mountain god.

Your serpent-god eyes, gleaming with the crystal clarity of the eagle, foretold the future. They saw the beyond. I am here, strengthened by your blood. I am not dead. I can still shout.

I shout, I am your people. You restored my soul, you gave me new tears, you gave orders that my wound should not heal, that it should grow more painful. From the day you spoke, from the time of your struggle against the iron-hard, bloodthirsty Spaniard, from the instant you spat in his face and your burning blood was spilled over the burning earth, peace and resignation were put out in my heart. Only fire exists. Only the serpent's hatred against the devils, our masters exists.

> *The river sings ,*
> *the lark is singing*
> *the wind blows in circles;*
> *The prairie grasses vibrate day and night*
> *our sacred river is roaring,*
> *the snow slowly melts and glows on the peaks of our*
>   *mountain-Wamanis, their teeth.*
> *Where have you been since they killed you for us?*

154

Our father, listen to the voice of our rivers and listen to the fearsome trees in the great forest. Listen to the furious and pristine song of the sea. Hear them, my Father, Serpent-God. We are alive! We drink a stronger blood, it grows more powerful from the rivers, from the stones, from the motion of the trees and the mountains. We rise up for your cause and remember your name and remember your death!

In the towns, little hearts, the children are crying with their
  little hearts
In the "puna" the men are without hats, without coats,
  almost blind,
the men are crying sad songs, their weeping is more sorrowful
  than the children's
Under the shade of the tree, Serpent-God, man is still crying,
his wound is greater than yours was, he is persecuted. Lines
  of lice.
Listen to the vibration of my body!
Listen to the cold which now rises in my blood, listen to its
  frozen tremor.
Hear the song of the dove on the "lambra" tree, the abandoned
  dove they never loved.
The sweet song of softly running rivers, song of the source
  quietly born into this world.
We are still alive, we are alive!

From your immense wound, from the pain that no one lessens, the anger boiling in your veins now rises for us. We will soon rise, Father, our Brother, my Serpent-God. We don't fear the bolt of gunpowder from our masters, their bullets and machine guns. We are not as afraid now. We are here! We shout out your name. We are like a swollen river, like a fire devouring the ripe hay, and like an endless multitude of jungle ants, we hurl ourselves into battle until our land is truly ours, until our towns are truly ours.

Listen to me, my Father, Serpent-God, listen to me:
their bullets are killing me,
their machine guns are making our veins burst,
their steel sabers cut through human flesh.
The crazed heavy hooves of their horses fitted in metal are

crushing my stomach
here and everywhere, on every cold flank of every hill,
  in Cerro de Pasco,
over the cold plains, along the steamy coastal valleys,
over the great living grasses, between deserts.
Everywhere.

Beloved little Father, Serpent-God, you, whose face is like the great sky, listen to me: the hearts of our masters are even more frightful now. Their hearts are dirtier and inspire more hatred. They corrupted our own brothers and have turned their hearts inside out. They've armed them with weapons evil itself could not have conceived. They are killing us. Yet there is great light in our lives! We feel resplendent! We have come down to the city of our masters. It is from here that I speak to you. Like an endless file of ants we have descended from the great jungle. We are here with you, beloved chief, unforgettable, eternal *Amaru*.

They took away our lands. Our little lambs must now feed on whatever dried leaves the wind blows, leaves that not even the wind wants for itself. Our one cow is dying and licks from the earth whatever salt is left. Serpent-God, our Father, in your days we were still masters, common owners of our lands. Now, like a dog running away from death we are descending into the warm valleys. We are terrified birds fanning out into thousands of foreign towns.

Listen to me, my father. We fled our faraway mountain-passes, we fled the cold, burning plains which the false *huiracochas* took from us. We fled from there and are now spreading ourselves over the four regions of the world. There are those who cling to their threatened, small lands. Those who stayed behind in their beloved homes are like us: they are shaking with anger and think and watch. We no longer have a death. Our lives are colder and more painful than death ever was. Listen to us, Serpent-God: the whip, jail, endless suffering and death, these have made us stronger. Like you, older brother. Like your body. Like your soul. To what extremes will this new life drive us? Strength ferments and grows in man because of death. Could that very strength not help man in stirring, in shaking the world?

I am in the immense village of Lima, head of the false *huiracochas*. I once lived in the *Comas* plain and I built my house on the sand, built it with my tears and my strength, with my own blood and all the while I was singing. The river which flows through my village and its shadows, a great wooden cross, all the grasses and flowering shrubs which surround my house are beating inside. There is a golden hummingbird playing in the air, suspended above the roof.

We have come to the immense village of our masters and are beginning to stir things up. We are reaching in with our hearts. We will go in. We will wrap our undying joy around the village. We will make a circle with the sparkling joy of the suffering man, master of all the powers in heaven. With our old hymns, with our new hymns, we are surrounding the immense village of our masters. With tears, with love and fire we will wash away the guilt accumulating for centuries inside the mercenary head of the false *huiracochas*. Whatever it takes! There are thousands upon thousands of us here. We are one. We have come together town by town, name by name and we are strangling this immense city which hates us, which feels the contempt of the horse's excrement for us. We will transform it into a city for men to intone the hymns of the four regions of our world, a city of joy where every man can work. We will turn it into an immense city that will not hate, a city clean like the snows of the mountain gods who live where the pestilence of evil never reaches. This is how it is, this is how it was meant to be, our Father, this is how it was meant to be, in your name, cascading over life like a waterfall of eternal waters, leaping and shedding light over our spirit, over the road.

Wait quietly,
listen quietly,
observe our world, silently.
I am fine: I will rise!
I sing.
I dance the same dance that you danced
I intone the same song.
I can already speak the language of Castille,
I understand the workings of the wheel and the engine;
your name grows with us,

José María Arguedas   157

we, the children of the huiracochas speak to you, we hear you,
we see you as the master-warrior, pure fire that shines and
  inspires.
Dawn is fast approaching.
They say that in other lands, beaten men, the ones that endured
  suffering, are eagles now, they are condors, masters of their
  own immense free flight.
Wait quietly.
We will go beyond anything you ever dreamed or wished.
We will hate more than you ever hated.
We will love more than you ever loved, with the love of
  the enchanted dove, love of the nightingale.
Wait quietly inside hatred, wait in restless, limitless love,
We will do what you could not do.
Frozen, sleeping lake, black precipice
blue fly that sees and announces death.
The moon, the stars, the earth,
man's soft but powerful heart ,
all those who live and do not live in this world,
wherever blood burns and wherever it doesn't burn,
  man or dove, stone or sand.
We will bring joy, that they may have infinite light,
  Amaru, my Father.
Holy death will come alone, no longer thrown at us
  in braided waves, no longer torn to pieces by a bolt of
  gunpowder.
The world will be man, man will be the world,
  everything in your measure.

Come down to this world, Serpent-God, infuse me with your breath, place your hands over the soft cloth which shrouds our hearts. Give me your strength, beloved Father.

KATATAY*

They say that the shadow of my people trembles,
it trembles because it is touching the sad shadow in the hearts
    of women.
Do not tremble, pain, pain!
The shadows of the condors are fast approaching!
– What brings the shadow here?
Is it here on a visit in the name of the sacred mountains?
Does it come in the name of the blood of Jesus?
– Tremble no more, do not stand there trembling.
This is not blood and these are not mountains:
it is the sun shining as it approaches riding on the feathers of the
    Condors.
– I am afraid, my father.
A burning sun beats down, it burns the cattle and hits hard on the
    women who are sowing.
They say that in the faraway mountains,
in the endless forests,
a hungry snake,
serpent-god made of gold, son of the sun,
is searching for men.
– It is not the Sun: it is the Sun's heart.
Its resplendence,
its powerful and joyful resplendence,
comes to us in the shadow cast by the eyes of the condor.
It is not the Sun, it is the light.
Rise, get on your feet, greet the eye without limits!
Tremble under its light,
shake with the trees of the great jungle,
Shout!
Form a single shadow, people, people of my land,
may all of us
tremble with the light that is coming.
Drink the golden blood of the god's serpent.
This burning blood is reaching the eyes of the condors,

* In Quechua: to tremble

it weighs down on the skies and makes them dance,
it forces them to come undone, to give birth, to create.
Go on creating, go on giving life, my father,
man, my equal, mine, beloved.

(I wrote this hymn upon seeing my brothers, residents of the town of
Ishua and Lima, dancing in a little room made from adobe, a dwelling
with a thatched roof set in an open field, at 1188 Av. Sucre, Pueblo
Libre, September 3, 1965.)

A CALL TO THE DOCTORS

To Carlos Cueto Fernandini
and John V. Murra.

They say that we know nothing, that we are backward, that our
heads will have to be replaced by better heads.
They say that our hearts do not suit the times, that they are full of
fears, full of tears like the heart of the lark, like the heart of a bull
when they sever its head: this is the reason for our heart's
impertinence.
This is what some doctors are saying about us, the very doctors that
fan out through our land and get fat and turn yellow.
Let them talk, let them prattle away, if that's what they like.
What are my brains made of? What constitutes the flesh of my
heart?
The rivers flow, they roar in the deep. Gold and night, silver and
night, they give form to rocks, to the cliff walls where the river
echoes: my mind, my heart, my fingers are made from that rock.
What do you not understand about the shores of the rivers, doctor?
Take out your binoculars, your best eye glasses and try to see,
if you can.
Five hundred types of potato flowers grow on the balconies that line
the cliffs. But your eyes can't see the lands where night and gold
and silver and daylight come together.
Those five hundred varieties of flowers are my brain, my flesh.
Why did the sun stop shining? Why have the shadows retreated from
everywhere, doctor?
Start up your helicopter and climb up here, if you can.
The feathers of the condors, the feathers of smaller birds have turned
into a rainbow and give out light.
The one hundred flowers of the *quinua* that I planted on the
mountain tops boil in colors under the sun. The condor's black
wing, the wings of the small birds have turned into flowers.
It is noon time and as I stand next to the sacred mountains, next to
the great snows their yellow brightness, red stain, is throwing light
into the sky.
On this cold land I plant *quinua* of a hundred colors. I sow one

hundred varieties of the powerful seed and those one hundred colors are the colors of my soul, of my untiring eyes.

Flapping my wings amorously I will extract the idiot stones from your brain. The stones are your downfall.

The unreachable echoes in the cliffs, the brightness of red snow keeps everyone away.

On your blood, over the apple of your eye I will spill the joyful juice of one thousand herbs, of one thousand thinking roots that can reason.

I will show you, brother, the heartbeat the thousand worms, keepers of earth and light. I will show you the clamor of flying insects, brother, and I will make you understand.

I will make you feel, I will make you hear the tears of the singing birds: their chests are soft like this dawn.

No difficult machines could teach me what I know, what I suffer, whatever rejoicing I draw from a joyful world.

We made all this out of the earth, we made this from the snow which breaks the bones, from the fire in the gorges. Before the sky, and thanks to the will of the sky, we made all this with our strength.

Do not go away from me, doctor, come up to me! Look at me, see me for what I am. How long must I wait?

Come closer, lift me up into the cockpit of your helicopter and I will treat you to spirits of one thousand different saps, I will treat you to the life of thousands of plants which I raised through the centuries, from the foot of the snows to the forests and the lairs of the wild bears.

I will cure you of the fatigue which clouds you like a bullet made of lead. I will recreate you with the light of one hundred *quinua* flowers whose image dances to the breathing of the wind. I will recreate you in the small heart of the nightingale, reflection of the world. I will refresh you with clean waters that sing, waters that I tear off the cliff walls whose shadows bring coolness to the creatures of this world.

Must I work for centuries of years and months so that some stranger will come and cut off my head with a small machine?

No, dear brother of mine. Do not lend your help to the sharpening of that machine working against me. Come closer, let me get to know you. Study my face carefully. Study my veins.

The wind which travels from my earth to your earth is the same wind, the same wind that we breathe.

The land you describe with your books, with your machines, with your flowers comes from my land, only it is improved, it is tamed.

Let them sharpen knives, let them thunder *zurriagos* let them knead mud and disfigure our faces. Let them do all that.

We are not afraid of death. For centuries we have drowned death in our blood and have made it dance over familiar and unfamiliar roads.

We know that they intend to disfigure our faces with mud, and show us off to our children so that they may kill us.

We do not really know what will become of us.

May death walk toward us. May the men we don't know come to us.

We will be waiting, standing on guard for them for we are the children of the fathers of all the rivers, of the father of all mountains.

Is this world not worthy of more, little doctor brother?

Do not answer. It does not matter.

Life is greater than the strength I have acquired over thousands of years, greater than the muscles I have built in my neck over thousands of months, thousands of years of strengthening.

This is life, this, my eternal life, the world that never rests, the world creating indefatigably, giving birth and shape like time does, without beginning and without end.

(1966)

RAISING A FLY

I am raising a fly
whose wings are made of gold.
I am raising a fly
with eyes of fire.

It brings death
in its fire eyes,
it brings death
in its hair of gold,
death rides its beautiful wings.

Inside a green bottle
I am rearing a fly:
no one knows
whether it drinks,
no one knows
whether it eats.

It wanders in the night
like a star,
it inflicts mortal wounds
with its red splendor,
with its fiery eyes.

There is love
in its fiery eyes,
its blood glows
in the night,
and the love it brings in its heart is glowing.

Nocturnal insect,
fly, carrier of death,
inside a green bottle
Ever lovingly
I nurture the fly.

One thing is certain:
no one knows
when I give it a drink
when I give it.

(1965)

I TURNED INTO A BUTTERFLY

I turned into a butterfly,
I went into your house
and touched your shadow.

You pretended not to recognize me,
and your feet crushed my little wing,
a part of my chest was broken.

Behold me now that there is no return for me,
now that I have neither wings nor chest to fly with.
I will turn forever under your shadow,
forever, tears in my eyes, sadness in my heart.

(1965)

Pablo de Rokha

Chile

1894-1968

DIAMOND TOY

Loneliness of the romantic hummingbird but the swallow's dramatic bodice and dual figure the crest of the baby heron in her eye rings they all belong to the Raimundo's beautiful girl

she is small like the immense fog which causes the sunset's seeds to grow she sobs and she resembles a sea chick on her bent knees and her compact in a to-and-fro of the world her chest with torn roses

and her little boots made of *queltegue* doing footwork on Raimundo Contrera's heart

over and over again Contreras feels that she did not happen from the outside to the inside like a ripe apple but from inside to outside like the fallen immensity of the future which is the past of hope and because he barely believes in the existence of his work he fills her to the brim with laments

he strips her of her clothes and find her indisputable

have you seen the sign being formulated by the river swinging the rump the rose tearful with pink shame?

Exactly the same as the sun agonizing as it mounts the earth

Raimundo wishes the black egg of night would burst forever like a timeless sea built from one infinity to another like this deep bed which ties them together embracing them with its dark honey so sharp spreading velvets like full lengths of tongues found dead in the yellows of our beloved beaches

the great melancholy beasts inside this provincial man surround Lucina they verify her they make her suffer and subject her to algid temperatures and she is encircled by the fires of dead dreams

and because Contreras stops roaring stops and scrapes in cemeteries and throws off historical shadows against confined doves and

searches and fells her total equation and piles on his bellowing all the
bulls in his ocean the caresses of his tongue like a dark beast's hallu-
cinations turn to gestures to songs to screams going back to those
proud elemental times Raimundo's little girl gets frightened and flees
and hides inside tenderness calling out for him from her daily chores
searching for him in her own premonitions in her condition as the
warrior's child fragrant with leafless dawns and Biblical lands

there are many innocent doves inside her eyes of fruit they nest
from one sky to another sky in the same manner as she formulates her
joyful flight but then he becomes sad and unhooks sunsets with a knife
stirring her hair in the great dawn

lion and dog anxiety the manner in which he obeys by sending love
licks passion bites and pulls the abyss against the wall of the storm a
sad thing no matter how joyful the brutality of the Jewish God an
exclusive diligent brutality hermetic like the fruit from the tree which
bears no fruit and is always burning with saintly obsession a fool
whose wound bleeds a bundle which resembles a star and is made
from blue suns the gesture of a triangular stone the yellow diamonds
inside that terrible pavilion mourning dragging along dead skies on
top of universes which are in lugubrious funereal order in the shadow
of shipwrecked vessels from a time when there was no time another
time which sings its frozen vanished attitude

the smell of stars enormously married to everything perfumes her
she is illuminated by the ancient sea flower and demonstrates a nest of
guitars in her mane unfurled in the joyful black wind seafaring gypsy
western dancer with her illustrious breasts of violets and a sugar tree
on her shores half-naked cherry garlic skin the smell of childish
woman

Lucina's little body growing with the great imperial roller coaster
the compass of high exiled souls great jewel made of mist crying on
the face of the poor forgotten gods among forgotten nations shaking
the ashes the crucifix of commitment with the infinite the precious
jewel of the hanged man of the judge and of the assassin and of all the
saints like a sign made of rubies or like the guillotine blade of a sword
owned by kings by thieves by sea captains or the glass beads of the

witch of the mad woman or the sweet mourning dove of dew singing as it flies among the under garments of a flower or plum breasts the finest the bluest the purest and most endearing of that endearing death of the young animal which bleats in the night mother of fright the anger of the genius a waistline made of stars or a poem of literary swallows the garters of the school girl

the ceramic style is a reminder of cocoa islands and flamenco – from Havana from Jamaica – brown skinned coffee pots and an Egyptian or Hebrew aroma of herbs of old books of geography's tall wide birds like poetry for the sedentary man a reminder of the oceanic sonority of rubber and molasses as well as the sunset and its peanut ever cheerful and burning reminding us of the happiness of sad beautiful parrots the tropical to-and-fro of canoes and palm trees and the sun and dancing the charleston and the colonial black flower and the tobacco's blond beard crying songs that sailors sing

Raimundo loves her and smells her like an orange but squeezes her too hard and she cries among sulking grapes and then he cuts roses of laughter and poppies for her

"he adores her" wants to kill her establish what is transitory within the absolute carve time carve the kiss into world-stone while possessing her against all things to last in that definitive instant eat the guts of all those who set eyes on her yes but something enormous surrounds her something made of sun and honey of ripe light ripe watermelon ripe guitar heart of saintliness

he looks at Lucina and remembers the deep persimmon tripe in the pots from Talagante the complete curve of humanity which illumi-nates its dramatic light with writing and with cemeteries

why do all the roads converge on Lucina? Because all the roads converge on Lucina as images converge on the poet and all the events and the conviction of this cosmic being surrounding her stance the adoring phenomena

Raimundo Contreras understands that his abandonment is diminished and begins to cry

(1929)
170

THE MAN WHO FORGOT ALL THINGS, OLD ABANDONED GOD

just like the creak of the wheel the mist is certain and a vague gesture indescribable Raimundo Contreras

has a face which twists toward the other side of the world

it seems that there are birds and birds and many birds around Contreras and that he hears cosmic dialogues and even that he died long ago in Mesopotamia crying for chilled stars and animals

this great smoke is Raimundo Raimundo is the blaze without fire without logs the same old problem with smoke poetry defeated and expanding in great waves blending into the incalculable blue

because Raimundo is round and he is not concave meaning re-sounding meaning that he covers his attitude like the hen throws God out on the first day of the most concave of mysteries similarly the sky's distraction is completely concave inside the distracted appear-ance rises in the four corners of the world shouting burning blue and situated next to absence

he takes Lucina as though she were a memory devoid of human matter like a fact or a dream he dreams about her or vice versa and he takes her as if one asked a cask about its contents and it answered through smell verifying the primordial truth of that cheerful murmur of years passed making wine boiling wine being the formidable that the bees make

there is a smile which reminds Contreras of the tides on the rocks and it is not he who smiles but all of him is a smile like the sun which does not sing but is song made of immutable song

''Lucina'' ''Lucina'' he stammers like someone calling the dove of forgetting and Lucina is kissing him like someone calling a dove moaning placing the honey at the threshold and he carries her within himself like sound inside the bell like any man who starts drinking the sky in great gulps and turns invisible to the light like bread eternal tune

you will walk for one thousand years for one hundred thousand years certainly Raimundo Contreras and Lucina

(1929)

SOUTH AMERICA

silver saint lives in electric geometry twisting driven by doves
without indicating the origin the adventure flags still silent moon still
so much moon of commerce for man for man still the married emerald
and the ship whose character cannot be demonstrated still the logic
whose walls are covered with cactus-fruit notwithstanding the strict
household with calendars from the radio-calendar good-byes are
possible they resemble the hurricane the electric violet little earthen
pot with leafy eyes snow now useless to grandpa resort doormats and
how the sincere *peumos* opposed to the charleston the urgent
adolescent ocean and dark whisky a face weeping in the wood I swear
on crossed dreams plowing the elegant philosophy of the railroads
spurring on the naked mares I am like the telegraphs just like the
guitars which resemble the sea and antiquity taken by surprise dove in
mourning in the evening covered in asphalt stars wearing episodic
wigs and inside the blond gramophones journalism lives and the
shimmy is full of cheer and soda little smoke face pyrogravure on
ordinary walking sticks that reach the only horizon while assuming the
attitude of a plucked monument whose simultaneous reasons are those
of grandiose pears falling or the milk below nailed turning huge
obsessive slice turning around the same thing toward the same gallop-
ing donkeys impressive *rajadiablos* kept under the oak trees in
concrete the globetrotter's lever strongly freely frankly red as the
sentimental songs of knife wielding thieves amusing the wounded
flower of sun like that pushing hard the cow the more the steel and
never and it's fine in the corkscrew against the sky above the assas-
sins the *boldo* trees are round and that great basin under the wet trees
of dawn like the joyful rivers the racetrack stretched over the bellow-
ing I behold the potatoes while I open up the bulging soil and the
alfalfa fields whose paint is so thick borders with advancing patterns
like the wheat fields like corn fields my sweet however the press
houses are boiling then the joy of crushed grapes fabulous the great
blue eggs and a happy gathering of haystacks noisy and pathetic
inheritance possibly the drama of the world...

(1927)

FUNERARY POETRY

Unquestionably, in rented houses,
on the shores of the bread and its peasant situation with a sun hat,
against big employees or those desperate,
and the terrible widows who let down their yellow structures of hair:
this is how we will die perhaps, howling against the mountain.

Having spent electricity and pants
sweating fear sweating the assassin's dignity ready to be shot by the
        terrified soldiers,
to witness with teeth full of mystery
the beloved turned to ruins, split apart by the years, enormously
        grand in her useless grandeur
squeezing her sad flesh against the walls,
or maybe she still fills up with flames as in the days of the peach
        when she was a dove,
and we looked at each other in front of a dead man.

People's hope is destroyed, the lily
and its shield are slowly eaten away by rust among the blue pots and
        the serious dead, a spectacle,
the desire within wears away
and urine and cemetery pound on this northern sepulcher,
        echoing like a bed.

Should have drunk,
should have drunk a few more casks of the principal red wine,
        substantial element of eternal bees,
should have owned the belt of the tribe's chief,
and that great bed stretching from this world to the next
there where the wild beasts grow,
funerary bees, panthers tormenting the guitar, lightning
and a large red sword
to help write the proletarian revolution,
and in the million sunsets
we took off our shoes, sobbing,
but the naked moon did not come
flowering forever to comfort the dying.

A human being. How does one pluck, how does one drown this
        simultaneity, the reflection of matter in the grave?
It turns lugubrious when the glands begin to fail,
deep inside man's liver the violets drop their petals.

One must possess heroism in order to agonize correctly,
with the eye's fingers and a dagger to pierce the accumulated mist
without giving up one's will to rot away.

Now, once we know how the soles of our feet rip through
        the sun's misery
once we have heard the tomb with its bullet,
gold and facts will constrict our throats.

If he buys a bronze bed, the bureaucrat will die like a worm
his tongue sticking out, surrounded by family
straightening out his simpleton's mind, like a bird, like a deer,
like the one who builds a house
and places it where things reach their conclusion.

All the lamps have gone out, the wind is dripping
and the sun assumes the shape of a funnel.

Only then will we understand the attacker the one who cut
        humanity's throat in order to buy laurels for his girlfriend,
the one who built his tribe on the public square while shouting
        with a steely voice
the one who ripped apart women and nations and rolled on the
        ground with a bolt of lightning, society with its stables of
misfortune,
and we will not understand each other because everything has been
        useless, everything is lost:
a suit made heroic by horror covers time eternal, forever the same
        quotidian nourishment,
dying on a mattress enormous, stupendous and afflicted,
pushing bitter third class wagons, pushing attempts, pushing canteens,
        pushing the abyss, pushing doves, forlorn,
because it is he and his heart who die, he will die
invaded by the powerful sands, by the ocean, by his gray horse and

the dark pearl that is inside the orange
no matter that his name be Luis or Domingo or Francisco.

   We who burned with happiness,
dragging our graves by the hair, will slowly decompose and turn
      to oil,
to nose, a worm, history
until we are left naked, without skin, without our insides and
without bones,
ourselves without ourselves,
just a hole of what we once were when we were the tongue itself,
when man was not
what he wanted to be, what he was to be – never –
turning also toward a dispersed life,
tired and dissatisfied like the idealist's horses.

   A single grape will equal a snake, an idea, or a paraffin yearling,
and the scorpion on the girls with their violet dresses,
or the religious spider will nest in the bird's cradle, undressing,
the trees will shed their leaves, events
will play the role of a falling leaf, yellow alphabet,
such heights, miserable soldier's bottle
the frightening need of having to grab on to one's own sighs,
scratching as we tumble down the mattresses
and agony begins with invasions of shipwrecks, immense floods,
the facts about furniture are lost and everything begins to turn into a
      totality which screams and rolls spinning on a vortex
where the dead man falls into his own skin.

   Roses on black and black people of the wind,
bitterness fermenting with good-byes, a storm of entrails the tears
the hair grows in the dark their screams.

   Let us not speak about a future made of sobbing
the city of the future organizing lime and cement with us,
and the atom's colossal loneliness
against us with its surroundings: its surrounding, oh, shipwrecked
      heart
intimacy unchained,

a scream never heard, a tenacious scream, a perishing scream of
        blood
regains its initial fear.

    It is not having ever understood within our bones
that substance is not us, our actions, our shoes, our loves, our senses,
        our ribs, our thoughts.
The eternal universe and society proclaim
historical-dialectical energy expressed in the person and the transience
        of people,
over these murky and dusty bundles
which could well be apples or heaps of gunpowder,
an afflicted habit, the hero,
the abandoned, the dark adjoining past in accumulated bureaucracies
the toil of toils, so many hard things and their pink chests
where we placed our powerful love and its whip – and its underwear
gives out a smell of seaweed –
because we embraced her nude, and it became more beautiful,
laughing, white as silver or as water, shaking her hair like a black
        flag unfurled in the deserts,
on top of this or that pile of terror where we die.

    Here is conscience and being, mixing burning trees and vistas
        to a song of the past
stirring brains and verse inside memory –a large space – and the dead
        man comes in
to the left, and the bird in the canticle of the elm trees in the cemetery
        struggling with us, we the worm-ridden, rotting like sardines
        stuffed like the caricature of a sad grocery store.

    Food tastes of death and our skin
smells of farewells and death and the whole business
the fruit, money, clothes, the grave,
and hammer and sickle brighten up our matter
like great steely houses on fire.

(1937)

SANCHO DIAZ, CAPTAIN OF THE
SOUTH DEFINES MAGIC ACTS

They are dead, surrounded by sardines and suet and doves
    and immortal neighborhood wine,
an enormous river flows through them, from the eyes to the mouth,
    wandering,
and they cry for the last button on the old vests, discolored flags and
    the god of the bottle and the coins, alone

Attacked by stumps covered in blood, by ghosts
surrounded, knifed, mugged, murdered, trampled on, eliminated, torn
    to pieces
by the walking stick and the mind's hell, oh unfortunate one!
bitten by heathen asses, by headless adventurers who inhabit
    his muscles,
dead man's kisses flowering between frightful snails.

Your country drowned and with it your earthen pitcher and the
    column
you will be sitting waiting for the foundation of the world, Sancho
    Díaz, waiting for the collapse of darkness,
the precise moment to attack furiously.

Talca, surrounded by stones, surrounded by a clan of anguish
    and stone, wrapped in yellow and in fright, wrapped in horror
hair and bones of our forefathers with their backs to us they eat a
    broken chain,
spoons and dentists and suitcases and bundles of madness and fearful
    belts running after ancient splendid toads
anguished sun and steel clamoring and the glass teeth, centuries old
scarecrows made of retired skeletons and seafood, living at the feet of
    the shipwrecked and pale men of hunger, fragrant genital horror
    and eagles,
solitude, immortality, so moribund,
the metal and the urine of love which is time and crown of myths...

What a terrible family wardrobe with its macabre and naked
    lesson of horror
and what subversive and pessimistic lice with their fiery tongues,
    going back in time riding on horseback in their despair,
while the rain greets everyone, hoisting its final farewell
from inside the black warehouses where habit is sewing a great
    shroud of felled orange trees and violets in the sun...

....

Dazzling and terrible, you raze the heads of the dead,
Sancho Díaz, the bats in your town roar like ancient swords in the
    dusty panoply
your voice gallops astride, on a dead lion,
and you are a soldier made of silver and stone with emptied eyes,
    the owner of a basket full of skulls,
hanging majestically from that skeleton, shining
before the horror of antiquity, a ghost puts out the centuries-old
    candlewith its sword
sparkling among foreign lilies.
Young provincial man, tremendously grown up with acacias and
    daggers,
the clamor of the dead rises in you
a great tear was strangled in your throat.

They all walk alone and the scorpion kicks them in the head,
in the common grave a lovely cow made of ebony gives birth to a
    child of glass who begins to cry terribly, who begins
to roar like a mountain, with its immense tongue,
the very instant when the headless bird licks the lantern of the
    world, its ill-smelling smoke.
Yes, by force, chained, convicts of pain, earth-colored
we are returning to ourselves, attacking terribly, we bite ourselves,
    we hurt ourselves, we eat our own raw guts
and the alcohol inside our hearts, this great flag made of mud kicking
    inside the guitar
among mourning faces and dead sexes, dog's hair, black cheeses, oh
    forlorn crowbar crying
immense mares suffering next to the louts,
the beds sigh the whole of history and the braziers and the vats

shake and sob against this year's empty moon
the dust shouts on someone's back, desperate, the sun collapses
     inside the bottles
and God's voice appears under the dust coats, God's voice: a coffin
     without its head,
fifty leagues from me everything remains the same
a creature made of hair, a faraway country, a country with vineyard
     skin, at once beautiful and universal, a country with as
     many birds as there are canticles,
only you, as though you were emerging from that which defines me;
yet, roofs and cattle and all the remoteness of all customs, the
     remoteness,
the remoteness of the present filled with so much of the past,
kite of love in worlds of rain, singing Pelarco's wet plucked
     songs,
the sea becomes discolored from the shipwrecks rises a song that is
absolute, unilateral, horrifying, a driving tune made of skeletons.

     ....

There is a magical, enigmatic quality,
because we are inside glass and time is motionless face to
     face with us while it reads its closed book,
and at this hour the world neither begins nor ends;
suddenly our sense of nature disappears and everything is in the
     present but is not current and it detonates dynamite,
horror's lion appears on the same shore of the universe,
all that we are and will be, what we were presents itself to us
     horribly, enormously, covered in fright's hair, toothless,
     horrendous and astronomical,
and emptiness opens its snout and barks at us, threatening us
from the beginning of time, a roaring chaos and the beginning of all
     things,
an alley with a candle at one end
at the end, a murdered god attacks us furiously, it moves its tail
     and the ears of its tail,
problems sink and destiny comes forth, its arms are severed
     and it trips
over its crutches, over a landscape full of gallows and crows.

....

Your supernatural pants, Sancho Díaz,
the magical life of your blind hair where the chains of the Egyptian
        or Hebrew heart once shone,
the eagles commit suicide and your yellow coffin
seizes my heart with its red and black scorpion crossing the sea,
        crossing
the sacerdotal desert of Mesopotamia.

And the first black-eyed song
and tenderness of disappeared coins,
velvet among watermelons and apples, bottle of memories, about
        memories, shedding her leaves like the cicada's funeral,
burning inside twenty lions, singing greatly naked here, fixing
the marvelous orange trees of our crumbling youth, making a huge
        racket
yes, as if running inside a silver ring,
tearing away from the sunset, extracting the teeth from her skull,
        surrounded by rotting sonatas
her laughter tears through, fragrant like the nuptial bed
her chest smells of stars, like the first time that I undressed her, like
        the first
invocation of mortality that the newlywed women intone,
and, in the collapse of bones and guitars and families and tenacious
        wines like the funeral of the world,
her head with its eminent ashes a reminder of the blackness of
        yesterday
the adolescent cry of the girl undressing among oranges and ponds.

....

Good-bye. The black sky, rigid, phenomenal, covers itself with
        gleaming corpses
and the great ghost is knocking at the open doors of the tombs
with a stick made of dust, with a point where a beheaded scorpion is

      roaring and above,
up above the past and the future, a petal
of eternity collapses bringing down the entire mountain of centuries
    past, Sancho Díaz, Captain of the South...

(1942)

César Dávila Andrade
Ecuador
1918-1967

ORIGIN

Now I know that I was given this soul at the height of battle.
Rendered mad by enemy torches,
I saw my mother's corpse under the Swan she loved.

I came to be different from the rest of you, Relatives
Minerals, Archangels.
My childhood never belonged to you.
I nourished myself alone like a mirror gone missing
deep in the forest.

My cradle was the banquet inside a mud-ball.
I devoured the knees of my wet nurse,
I soaked up the long eyes of the women watching as I came
	out of the angel
and I was accepted dressed in the garments of the white caterpillar.

Surrounded by distant hosts and hereditary names,
	I struggled,
covered in the blood of Mercy and Crime.
(Oh that terrible eve of my coming into the World with those
	condemned to die.
The Almighty's enthusiasm ends in matter.)

My mother would travel equal distances in the room.
A man lying on the saints' flat berth
was aging before and after me.
He drank his coffee deeply
as though he were dying in gulps;
he combed his hair with a comb made of smiling bone
and watched his corn-wood coffin.

And the horror ran down the rain laden sides of the school.
Mass loaded with wood and fire like a ship.
The little bell in the four corners of the room
like dew which flies away when threatened.

Those holidays, never to return.
I hid my leather-lined book bag in the barn.
I wore a blue hat at the bottom of the photograph,
walked in a forest of paper during a literary evening,
a mountainous December day.
Good-bye.

Those holidays! We would go out to the fields.
But before,
the dog would walk straight to a hidden flower and wet it
standing with one leg on a difficult spot of paradise.
Those brief spikes biting at my mother's skirts
followed her to bed.

While the night lasts,
the prettiest rubble walks across the fields.
The trees remain unseen as they lean down
to pick up the lightly moist arrows that bring them joy.
Old bulls ruminate inside their sphinxes,
the old muleteers converse with sleepless horses
before dawn comes and destroys them.

Innocence, you were longingly gazed at by the large eyes
of domestic animals
just dismounted from coitus
with the sadness of deceived farmhands.

My fathers:
I know that inside your ceremonial glass,
behind the children's backs
you engage in the miserable pastimes of the flesh
which merely bring you shame each morning.

Your hands, my fathers,
smell like those skins the Ocean washes on the beach:
Good-bye

Your lashings
will be a memorable souvenir

on the dark buttocks of Indian servant girls,
like the hide of a zebra shaken by lightning bolts
Good-bye.

Take good care of the hay, of the common lands,
of the graves;
Look after public electricity which prolongs its acid globes
over our people's huts
on Saint John's Night.
Good-bye.

Behold:
Our father's seventh wife is already undressing.
Her pubic hair is the black ace of hearts on the bed.

Acts of divination take place where the doors thin out.
Listen:
The adults are arriving and will drown in the white flood waters
    of their sheets.
Here they come to chain us down until dawn.

We leave.
We are born in successive skies,
inside the plumage that the Old Sower throws over the Queens.
But we wake up all the poorer,
with the light that filters through the thin grooves of the hand
like a beautiful face known to us one thousand years ago.

I also dreamed.
I saw a woman accumulating rolls of purple cloth
around the pale rod of her soul.
I addressed myself to the young idolatresses who polish their throats
before drowning in the theologian's pond .
Sad clowns dug into the flour of their skin
in order to show me their imploring ulcers.
I saw the dwarves stumble
under the wings of women skaters
I heard the roar of the tea that those sad shipwrecked Captains
drink on their final evening.
I saw columns stammering before the sun.

One hundred eras ago
I lived a mysterious instant of love which I have now forgotten.
I am no longer that man. Waves of time in Time passed
I was called into the confines of our Elders,
and I was entrusted with my shadow.
I am no longer the man you used to hide in the Ovary
of the Great Sitting Statue
during those rainy afternoons of the Ecuadorian South!
I am no longer the man you used to hide under a cloud of false
    witnesses,
while the woman went by naked and tousled,
she who flies over the eyelids of adolescents.

Someone must continue to be tied down by the hair
that grows from the source of our Savage Mother.
Someone must continue to write on the dust with his finger.
Someone must continue to hunt the parrot
in the leafless sky.
Someone must continue the song of The Chiaroscuro Man of Night.
Someone must prolong the agony of our Elders
on the wandering table covered with a handkerchief of corn.

(1962)

OH, WE LIVE SURROUNDED
BY INSECTS

Oh, we live surrounded by insects and difficult hymns!
Under trees felled by mistake we hear the storm of the day upon us,
we listen to the trees blowing their ruin into a clay conchshell

In the corners of the rooms the girls fill up with motherhood.
Our sisters don their long stone dresses
before leaving for the *quina* tree mountains.
A man I met had a lascivious princess
tied to a pig, worn as meaningful adornment on his vest.
Up the mountain go the Indians carrying
the dark candelabra they will use in the terraces of the Apocalypse!
The wretched man pedals down the last Sunday of our times.
The solitary bull climbs up and dies inside a frozen Inca temple.
Children hang from the stake's bosom like livid fish.
Thousands of drunken men lean over to drink mystery
from the cradles' thirsty cracks.
Women hide and weep behind the bird's heart.

I name the city. I shout it out. I express my love for its stones,
for its crests, its little doors leaning on two walking sticks!
But no one answers! Like me, someone writes on the grass
his simple poet's epitaph.

I go out. I go for a walk at night in the company of dogs sharpened
     by the moon.
I listen – in horror– to things beating over the hollow decimals
which have made them one with the abyss for two thousand years.

I hear the waters of the End licking
their sleepy gentlemen!
I hear the steps of mortal products wandering among the beds
     of the wretched ones.

I hear the sounds of love leaping in moist couples, like toads.
Secretaries and pimps sleep.
They march down naked to greet the great crash of dawn!
While they sleep their faces take on the deformed
appearance of anguish of the animals that they train.

NEIGHBORHOOD

Sometimes I look at those white garments made for crying
which hang in the balcony of the Virgin Mary.
She might be going into town to get oil or flour,
or to kill the time she's got left
until she can ride sure-footed on the stirrups of Paradise.

During the afternoon I hear the sounds of a clavichord
on which a girl is learning to play music.
And she is like the blind woman on the Moon.
Every one hundred years she takes
the severed hand of another girl,
dead before Genesis.

Day after day I look at my chain
coiled at the bottom of a drawer
I address her thus: "Mother, mother, I love you"
She moves her tail lovingly:
Out of tenderness the snake grates and gnashes.

(1959)

BULLETIN-ELEGY FOR THE "MITAS"*

I am Juan Atampam. I am Blas Llaguarcos, Bernabé Ladña, Andrés
    Chabla.
I am Isidro Guamancela, Pablo Pumacuri, Marcos Lema, Gaspar
    Tomayco.
I am Sebastián Caxicondor. I was born and I endured my suffering at
Chorlavi, in Chamanl, in Tanlagua
Niebli. Yes I suffered greatly in Chisingue, Naxiche,
in Guambayna, Paolo and Cotopilaló.
Blood and sweat at Caxaji, Quichirana,
in Cicalpa, Licto and Conrogal.
Endured Christ's suffering for my people at Tixán, in Saucay,
in Molleturo, in Cojibambo, in Tovavela and Zhoray.
This is how I gave more whiteness and pain to the Cross brought over
    by my executioners.
The drum beats for me. The drum beats for José Vacancela.
For Lucas Chaca the drum beats for Roque Caxicondor, the drum
    beats.
At the Square in Pomasqui standing in a circle with the other locals,
they sheared our heads down to cold.
Oh, Pachacamac, Lord of the Universe,
your smile felt more frozen than ever in those days,
and up the high wastelands we climbed with our naked heads,
and crying we crowned ourselves with your Sun.

To Melchor Pumaluisa, son of Guapulo,
made to stand in the middle of the hacienda's courtyard:
with a knife for cutting pigs open
they cut off his testicles.
And they kicked him and they made him walk
before our tearful eyes.
Blood pouring out of him in fits and starts.
He fell face down on the flower of his body.
Oh, Pachacamac, Lord of the Infinite,
You who stain the sun as you walk among the dead...

* "Mitas" in Quechua: Tribute paid by the Indians to a landlord

And your Lieutenant, Head Justice
José de Uribe: "I order you." And I
and the other Indians, at his beck and call, we took him
from house to house, carried him on a hammock when he
    wanted to stroll.
While our women, our daughters, *mitayas*,
were ordered to sweep, to card and weave, to pull out weeds,
to spin, to lick the earthen dishes – of our own making –
our flowers, both their thighs,
forced to lie with *Viracochas*
and give birth to half-breeds, our future executioners...

Without pay, without corn, without *runa mora*,
no longer hungry from so much hunger,
mere skull, old frozen tears of sorrow running down my cheeks,
arrived carrying fruit from the *yunga*
with four weeks of fasting inside.
I was greeted by this: My daughter split in half by
Lieutenant Quintanilla.
His common-law wife. My sons whipped to death.
Oh Pachacamac, and I, to Life. This is how I died.

And because of this pain and to the seven skies
and to the seventy suns, oh, Pachacamac,
I twisted the arms of the woman who bore my son,
Sweet from so much miscarrying, she said:
"Break the baby *maqui.*" I do not wish
it to serve the *Viracochas* as peon. I broke the baby.

And among the priests, some resembled devils, vultures.
One and the same. Worse than the two-legged ones.
And the others were saying: "Son, Love, Christ."
In the churches we were made to weave, and the oil for the lamps,
wax for the momuments and eggs of ash,
doctrine and blind catechisms.
A guitar, an Indian woman in the kitchen, a daughter in the house.
They spoke. I obeyed.

And later: Sebastian, Manuel, Roque, Selva
Miguel, Antonio, Matiyos: grass, firewood, coal,
hay, fish, stones, corn, women, daughters. All the services.
For you man-fire, you who ate two thousand of their hearts
     in three months.
To the woman that you ate,
within hearing distance of her husband and her son,
night after night.

The arms lead us to evil.
The eyes to our crying.
Men were lead to the breath of the whip,
their cheeks placed under hard boots.
Their hearts were squeezed and stomped before the *mitayos'* eyes,
bodies of mothers, women, daughters.
Only we have suffered
the horrible world of their hearts.

In sweatshops for the making of fabrics, twills, capes, ponchos.
I, naked, sunken into my cell, I worked
a year forty days,
hardly a fistfull of corn for the pulse
thinner still than the thread I was weaving.
Locked up from dawn till next daybreak,
with nothing to eat, I weaved and weaved.
I who wove what the bodies of my Masters wore
and the weavings brought white loneliness to my skeleton.
When Good Friday came, I woke up: locked up,
face down on the loom,
blood vomit between threads and shuttle.
Thus, with my soul full of my side, I dyed
the clothing of those who stripped me bare.

   Because we have not come
   to live in this world.
   Only to dream
   here on Earth.

And they brought a Christ intentionally,
hidden in their lances, flags and horses.
And in his name they made me thankful for my hunger,
for my thirst, for the daily lashes, for the church service,
death, for the stripping of race from my race.
(Warn the world, Friend of my anguish.
Warn the world. Give. Give by speaking out. God bless.)

And under that very Christ
came a black cloud of rag vultures. So many.
Hundreds of haciendas and houses built on our Motherland.
Thousands of children. Thefts at the altar. Knavery in bed.
They left me stranded on a road,
going neither South, nor North, not to a hut, nowhere. They left me.
And later, sent to beat the mud, the guts of my homeland,
sent to make lime from limestone, to work in the mills,
in the temples and its walls, paintings, columns and capitols.

And I, at the mercy of the elements!
And later, in the sugar mills,
I ground sugar cane and ground down my hands:
my laborer brothers drank from my ''saguanza''
Honey and blood and tears.
And they, who numbered so many, in the taverns
taught me about the sad heaven of alcohol.
and despair. Thank you!

> *Oh Pachacamac, Lord of the Universe!*
> *You who are neither woman nor man.*
> *You who are Everything and who are Nothing,*
> *listen to me. Hear me out.*
> *Like a deer wounded by thirst,*
> *I am searching for you, I adore only you.*

And the drum beats, my Friend, if only you knew about my anguish
and how they whipped me each day for no reason.
''Cape to the floor, underpants to the floor,
you, face down, *mitayo*. Start counting the lashings''
And I counted: 2, 5, 9, 30, 45, 70.

That is how I learned to count in the Castilian language,
through my pain, through my wounds.

I would get up right away, blood dripping down,
forced to kiss the whip and the hand of my executioners.
"Thank you in the Name of God, Dear Master" – I spoke out of
    terror and gratitude.

One day in the holy church of Tuntaqui
the old parish priest showed me the body on the cross:
Master Jesus Christ,
the only naked *Viracocha* without spurs and without a whip.

All of Him, one great splattered wound.
No room left to place a leaf of grass
between wound and wound.
First they set upon Him, then on me.
Should I complain? – No. I merely speak.
They hurled me. They tormented my body
with a red-hot iron.
They sheared me. I became the child of fasting and exile.
They wounded me with burning *maguey* tinders.
After the lashings, while still on the ground
They beat me with two smouldering candle brands, alternating them
they covered me with a rain of pointed sparks
which made the blood in my ulcers screech. Like that.

Among the women dishwashers, sweepers, herbalists,
one woman who went by the name of Dulita dropped her clay bowl,
and down it came in one hundred pieces.
And the half-blood Juan Ruiz urged on by all that hatred for us,
because of his twisted blood. He arrived.
He took her into the kitchen kicking her on the buttocks, and she did
not cry a single tear. She merely uttered a word which belongs to her
    and to us: *Carajú.*
And the coward, he put an eggshell in the fire
turned it into white ember almost and pressed it against her lips.
They opened into a fruit of blood. Next morning she woke up
    with sickness.

Did not eat for five days, and I and Joaquin Toapanta de Tubabiro,
found her dead in the sewer ditch.

And high up there, a wandering
cow, a veal or a sheep died
killed by vultures or just by life,
I was to drag it down leagues of grass and mud
to the hacienda's courtyard
and show its corpse.
And you, Lord Viracocha,
you forced me to buy that meat crawling with worms. And since I
could not even afford to pay
for the worms put together,
you forced me to work another year
until I myself went down to join the worm
that devours master and *Mitayo*.
To Tomás Quitumbe from Quito who fled
in terror into the hills of *sigses* of silver and feathers:
they went after him, a second lieutenant leading the pack.

And he ran moaning like a deer.
But he fell down, his feet torn by so many stones.
They hunted him down. Then they tied him by the hair to
    the tail of a colt
and then to the sweatshops at Chillos,
dragged him along ditches, stones, brambles and hardened mud.
When they came to the courtyard, they filled his wounds with salt and
hot pepper,
just like that: all over his sides and his shoulders,
    his arms and thighs.
Rolling on the floor he moaned: "Master Viracocha, Master
    Viracocha."
No one heard him die.
And mamma Susana Pumancay, from Pnazaleo,
her hut among reeds and thousands of fluttering butterflies.
Because her husband Juan Pilataxi went away
when she was pregnant they took her to the hacienda,
to the torture room, where they tortured her from the right
while they left her left side on the rack.

And she, she gave birth at midnight,
in a pool of water and blood.
And the baby hit his head against the wood and died.
He might have drunk silver milk one day, *caraju*!
I was a miner, two years and eight months.
Nothing to eat. Nothing to love. Never life.
The pithead was my heaven and my grave.
I, who had worn gold only on my Emperor's holidays,
had to learn to suffer its light,
because of the greed and the cruelty of others.
Thousands of *mitayos* sleeping,
nothing but flies and lashings, feverous inside the sheds,
watched over by a master who parceled out death.
But after two years and eight months, I left.
Of the twenty thousand who went in
only six hundred of us *mitayos* came out.
But I did come out. Oh sun, blown up by my mother!
I will say to you, oh *Pachacamac*, dead
in the arms of that other God
cornered in wood and nails.
I came out. And when I did I no longer knew my Homeland .
From blackness, I went back to blue
Quitumbe made of sun and soul. I cried with joy.
We came back. I had never been so alone before upon coming back.
Among the *cumbe* caves, a few water drops away from Cuenca,
Alive with moon, I found the corpse
of Pedro Axitimbay, my brother.
I stared at him for a long time and found his chest.

Flattened bone. Mirror. I leaned over.
I saw myself, blinking. And I recognized myself. I was
    the same person.
And I said: Oh Pachacamac, Lord of the Universe!
Oh Chambo, Mulalo, Sibambe, Tomebamba,
Guangara of Don Nuño Valderrama.
Good-bye. Apachacamac. Good-bye Rimini. I will not forget you!
You, Rodrigo Nuñez de Bonilla,
Pedro Martin Montanero, Alonso de Bastidas,
Sancho de la Carrera. Diego Sandoval.
My hatred. My justice.

César Dávila Andrade   197

For you, Rodrigo Darcos, owner of so many mines,
owner of the lives of so many *curicamayos*.
The laundering places you own by the Santa Barbola river.
The Ama Virgin of the Rosary Mines in Cñaribamba.
The mines in the great mountain at Malal, next to the frozen river.
Mines at Zaruma. Mines at Catcocha. Mines!
Great seeker of wealth, demon of gold.
You who suck the Indian of his tears and his blood!
The Indian watching over your watering ditches for a hundred nights
the same Indian who will grind your gold for you in mortars
    with eight hammers
Gold for you. Gold for your women. Gold for your kings.
Gold for my death. Gold!

But one day I came back. I am back now!
Now I am Santiago Agag Roque Buestende,
Mateo Comaguara, Esteban Chuquitaype, Pablo Duchinachay,
Gregorio Cuartatana, Francisco nati-Cañar, Bartolomé Dumbay!
And now all of this land belongs to me.
From Llangagua to Burgay,
from Irubí to Buerán,
from Guaslan to Punsar by way of Biblián.
I own it inside, woman in the night.
I own it upward beyond the sparrow hawk.

I have come back! I will rise up!
I rise up from among the Dead after three centuries!
I arrive with the Dead!
The Indian grave writhes with all its hips,
its breasts and wombs.
After three Centuries, the Great Tomb
arches and rises out of the hills and the barren plains,
it rises out of the summits, out of the warm valleys and the abysses,
it rises from among mines, sulphur and *cangaguas*.

I come back from the mountains where we used to die
under the cold's light.
From the rivers where we crowded in to die.

From the mines where we would die in rosaries.
From Death where we died inside the grain.

I am coming back.

We have come back, Pachacamac!
I am Juan Atampan! It is I!
I am Marcos Guamam, yes it is me!
I am Roque Jadán, I , yes I!

I am Comaguara, Gualanlema, Quilaquilago, Caxicondor,
Pumacuri, Tomayco, Chuquitaype, Gartatana, Ducninachay,
Dumbay, I am!

We are! We will be! I am!

(1957)

A WARNING FROM THE EXILE

One day, when you set out to look for me,
stay by the door.
Shout at the top of your lungs the name of one of your people.
I will answer by opening the ground
with the help of one of my weak ribs or a memory.
I who am here, sleeping perhaps
I who have yet to arrive, who have yet to wake up,
I who have gone beyond the day of exile.

Shout yesterday's name but make it sound eternal.
Make it sound of Never, like an uncreated angel.
Make it sound of Nothing, like a head turned upside down.

I will answer: "Past present."

I deny myself because when I find myself I suffer.
I come from yesterday, from last night, when dead.
I come from yesterday, from a past which already feels eternal.

It is true that I came down one morning
with salt's name between my lips
and a stain of sky on my soul.

It is true. But my great secret
was never where my name was.
Today I remember my days among other peoples.
The old Law and the gold of the herd,
when through the shepherd's crook my pulse felt
the simultaneous origin of the grass.

I come from yesterday and I visit myself today
because of some carelessness where the Eternal sat down and wept.

(1959)

200

Gonzalo Rojas
Chile
1917

TO SILENCE

Oh voice, only voice a great hollowed sea,
the totality of the hollowed sea would not suffice,
the sum of the hollowed sky
the whole recess of beauty
would be insufficient to contain you
even if man were to be silenced and the world were to sink
majestic one, you would never,
you would never cease to be in all places
because you have time and life to spare, unique voice,
because you are here and you are not here, and are almost my God
and are almost my father when I am darker.

AGAINST DEATH

I tear off these visions and I tear out my eyes with each passing day.
I do not want to see, I do not wish to see people dying every day.
I would rather be made of stone, turn into darkness
and not withstand the disgust of turning soft from within while I
  smile
left and right in order to prosper with my business.

I have no other business than to be here telling the truth
in the middle of the street, shout it out to the four winds:
the truth of being alive, just alive,
with my feet on the ground, with my skeleton free to roam the
  world.

What good will come from having reached the sun with machines
that move at the speed of our thoughts and our demons?
What will result from flying beyond the infinite?
We go on dying without any hope of living
outside this dark time.

God is of no use to me. No one is of any use to me.
Yet I breathe and I eat and I even sleep
thinking that I still have some ten or twenty years left before I fall
headlong, asleep like all the others under two meters of cement

I do not cry, I do not cry for myself. Everything will be as it must be,
yet I cannot stand and watch as box after box
passes, passes and passes minute after minute,
full of something, stuffed with something. I cannot look
at the blood still warm inside those boxes.

I touch the rose and kiss its petals. I love
life and do not tire of loving women: I find nourishment
in the world which opens up inside them. It is useless
because I myself am a useless head
ready to be severed, unable to understand
why we should expect another world from this world.

They speak to me of God or they speak to me of History. I laugh
at having to look so far afield for an answer to the hunger
that devours me, this hunger of living like the sun
inside the grace of the air, forever.

COAL

I see a swift river shiny as a knife cutting
my Lebu into two fragrant halves. I hear it,
I smell it I caress it and cover it with a childish kiss like
   in days of old
when wind and rain rocked me I can feel it
like another artery between my temples and my pillow.

It is him. The rain is falling.
It is him. My father is approaching. He is drenched in the fragrant
wetness of his horse. It is Juan Antonio
Rojas mounted on a horse crossing a river.
Nothing new. The torrential night collapses
like a flooded mine trembling with lightning.

Mother, he will be here soon. Let's open the gate,
give me that light. I want to be there to greet him
before my brothers. Let me take him a good glass of wine
to help him recover so he can embrace me with a kiss,
so I can feel the barbs of his beard piercing my skin.

Here comes the man, here he comes,
covered in mud, angry at misfortune, furious
at exploitation, he is starving, fast approaching
under his Castilian cape.

Oh, immortal miner, this is your house.
Yours are the hands that built these oak walls. Come in:
I am here waiting for you. I, the seventh
of your sons. It does not matter
that so many stars have crossed the sky in the last few years,
that we had to bury your wife one terrible August,
because you and she have multiplied. No matter
that the night was just as dark
for you as it was for me.
         – Come in, don't stand there
watching me, not seeing me under the pouring rain.

DIVINATION

Open the left hand wide, stretch out your thumb. Everything
has been written down by the knife: licentiousness
and strictness, motionless days
turbulent days give form to this network
and the sad, sad girl is crying. Identity:
one in three. Do you understand? A long childhood
and the broken star. Trips, trips
and more trips; the accident that night
in Madrid. Honors, many honors.
Blows of the rudder, a terrible punishment
till you bled, so much bleeding. More change
under the protection of Jupiter, Jupiter always, growth
far into the future with your two children, here is – close
that wild hand! – the stroke.

TWO CHAIRS BY THE EDGE OF THE SEA

The chair feels overwhelmed by the liberty with which the other
chair on the beach keeps watching,
closely scrutinizing,
a violation out in the open
on the dirty sand at dawn. Yesterday
was Sunday and now the crystal is broken.
The other chair is
feeling overwhelmed
by this chair.

They are stick and canvas of what they were
last night at the party, tousled stick and canvas now
they who once probably danced all white
and beautiful until the other
ate from the one and the one
from the other out of frivolity, until Zeus came
and skinned them like two she-asses
without lineage only to film them, fix them to the spot
until the end of Time, stiff, skinny
and lazy.

AIR TABLE

If we consider the imagination to be an invention,
which in fact it is, and we consider the great house made of air,
which we call Earth to be an invention. And if this fragile, salty
mirror conceived in our image and likeness were to reach
the beyond, if it were
invention of inventions, and if my mother
dead and sacred were an invention surrounded by irises,
and all the wandering waters
of the oceans which flow
like a secret from that deep,
beautiful source of matter were an invention,
and instead of rope and asphyxia, breathing were
an invention and the movies, the stars, music,
anger and suffering, if Revolution
were an invention, if the very
air table on which I write were no more than
an invention writing these words on its own.

OUR DEATHS SEEM TO BE
LINKED TO MANNEQUINS

Our deaths seem to be linked to mannequins,
frightened and motionless in the window,
horizontal and impudent
as if one were something other than this,
under carnations and gladioli made from wire
because of the misleading lights,
                              a strange salt
takes over then
and from the fingernails to the eyelids we
begin to grow in phosphorous resurrection.
                              Adverse
circumstances prevent me from attending.

I GET UP AT FOUR O'CLOCK

I get up at four o'clock and make sure that the air is still there,
that stone and air are one. Thanks to prison discipline
I am able to get up in two speeds. Conviction works and I am up
in one leap. And whom should I meet
when I step into the street but Magdalene.
Magdalene is the first person I run into
crying. – Come in! – I say
– don't just stand outside, sacrificed. The seven
demons in her body are no longer there.

    She
looks at me, perhaps
she is looking at me, comparing me
to the Other and she withdraws into herself. Yet
what we have here is not an apparition dressed
in a state of grace emerging almost naked
from of her feet, but the very same
ancient and mad Hebrew woman with unbound hair
disguised as the whitest of white cats,
lost in the night, badly injured
by love.

SHAVINGS

For some years I have been watching this shaving of light
near the left cavity, between the wing
of my nose and my eye; suddenly,
– it may seem like an obsession but it is not an obsession – I speak
and it flies, it sparkles
like a knife. No, it is not a butterfly. It does have something
of a butterfly, but it is not a butterfly.

It settles there and sleeps for hours on end
vibrating like a sitar. It is then
that I resort to the mirror. – Let's see, mirror –
I say – let's discuss
this phosphorous stain. The mirror laughs,
winks at me, the mirror laughs.

It is because of deprivation, it has everything to do with privation.
A year after being born one already feels like one should take one's
    leave.
The question is, where?
and this is where the game
of transference begins. I want this eye to be a hand,
protests one, but not just a hand. Let it be air: that is
what I want: to be made of air. How is it that the water
in the clouds is air?

Therein lies the explanation for shavings: old age does not exist,
old age cannot be. We have just arrived.
Wherever we arrive, at whatever hour, we are just arriving.
When we bet everything and lose everything we are just arriving.
When we love, when we engender, we are just arriving, when we die
falling down the stairs, we are just arriving.

All this without insisting on the person. What is a person?
Who has seen that person? Of course, there is a bed
and someone slept in it, a speck
of blood on the window, a hole

on the glass and one meter away in its lethargy, the mirror:
    the great mirror
with no reflection.

TO ANDRE BRETON'S HEALTH

Defunctus adhuc loquitur

And the Fly was saying, the Fly was saying that it is not such a big
deal, it's never such a big deal, the nose
is not for breathing and we will all burst:
tel qu'en lui-même enfin l'étérnité le change.
See you in the twentyfirst century, if you come back. The comedy
is over and the ocean and the lost fish.

And the Fly was saying, this is what Fly said: let's put this dead man
on the block.
How much for his millenial lion's head,
his Etruscan arrogance and his ivory airs?
How much for his mistakes? Dance, snake, dance.
Or else this volcano with its old ashes will sink.

There you go, running down in the *moving truck*, oh Paris,
lucid inside your diamond. And we say: Wait for us.
We will cover you with petals on this dirty November.
   But we could not.
Lilacs of rain to bid you farewell.
Right there, where Nadja is crying, the enigma.

— *I do not come from The Pond, beauty will be convulsive,*
   I denounce all followers,
or will not be, life is in the lightning bolt.
To run, to run by running up the stairs. I will cut the highest point of
   asphyxia's artery,
and the broken mirror, I am glass, this blood is me on the ground:
   ready to drip.
I've come back just to say that nothing, that never, that we are born.

All of the writings in the world owe you, and the oxygen,
the madness of reason and the stormy sea owe you,
eye and hand owe you, the glass in all things, freedom,
pregnancy, childhood, the nine larvae
of chaos: suddenly we are alive.

— They locked me up in this pen, in this village, our planet, they
threw me into
a straitjacket, they shaved my head. I can't stand it any longer! The
roses! My Word was
stolen from me, cut short. Revolution! I kiss with rage.
I was going to tell you quickly, but the fleeting phoenix!
But never, but tomorrow, but suddenly...

And mad love, all the mad love
of the naked ones, the Howler.
Craters, our senses, everything opens and closes and that mad,
    mad love.
We come from the dust, from the smell of the knife, from the kiss
of this woman and this man, and the air, the air, the air,
so that only one may come and may write on
the other side of the to-and-fro of things, the open pentagram,
    and we are waiting
for the sun and the last seer among us,
a condor without a mother: No one, yet everyone and everything, as
the days on this earth go by
and the game has been played, and the terrible tables.

(1966)

Aldo Pellegrini
Argentina
1903-1973

SONG

I hear your ancient song, your song and the lineage of your eyes
a song of hidden places
a song for your brow and for your veins
and for sonorous hair
song that shakes the subterranean beings
and fills the space with its music.

Your body resounds in the silence
like a great organ whose vibrations
are the music of madness which seizes
the stranger living in me.

Where and in what unavoidable names are you anchored?
You rest before the fountain of death
murmurs of silk surround you
and rise up the infinite stairs
until extreme weariness knocks them down.

Candid
benign forehead,
what names can I use to call you, hidden one?
In what palaces, in what corners will I not search for you ?
What shadows, what strange hands will I not rescue you from?
There are silences covered by the dust that the drunken butterflies
leave behind.

Furrow of your wounds where the blood never flows,
you hide behind smiles
the fruits born of your eyes dry up
they advance toward the final desert of patience.

Tear off your mask of ice, blow and set the wind on fire
martyrs and travelers whirl
around this season bristling with your fury.
There is no escape for anyone.

A warm day envelopes us
as I take refuge
in your shadow
the future is slow, everything falls asleep
with the to and fro of a wild pendulum.

(1952)

THE TRANSPARENT WOMAN

Your voice was a drink I sipped in silence.
Before astonished gazes
a bird of light
came out of your transparent body
a bird of light
            a fluttering instant
a vertiginous speed
which crosses one street after another
and follows your fleeting body.
When will you leave that mad pack of dogs behind?
Forlorn,
you tore yourself apart as you fell
and the remains of your body now drag themselves through the four
    corners of the world.
Yes, one day you will be reborn you,
            oh transparent one,
unique, unmistakable
leaning slightly, never falling,
surrounded by an impenetrable silence,
advancing with your fragile foot and surrounded by a vacillating
    monotony.
Yes, one day your laughter will be reborn
a laughter like a transparent bird,
your wounded laughter.

(1949)

THE WOLF BORN OF LOVE

The one who is given his daily bread
knows how to conceal it during his nights of philosophical bitterness
every thought is a curtain to the heart
the traitors gather the crumbs at the lovers' banquet
that was when love was not known
those sacred lips shed light on the sinister eyelid
an oblique eye which went down to the bottom of the innocuous heart
a love born of love and everything became clear
the newly arrived got up respectfully
and greeted the three empty udders
love made a convenient appearance and destroyed all hope
those who did not want to hear became aware of love and the
    gravedigger bowed down
drunk hagglers carried fragile love toward an endless time
and this is how it was shattered as it fell from the height of the lost
    glance
it shattered with the din of a lightning bolt of sugar
and there was an empty bite
in the great black hole of love.

(1957)

ON THE VARIOUS FORMS OF PLEASURE

A piece of paper
a tree walking out to meet the glance
an inscription on a virgin's breast
an expression of contempt which turns faces to liquid
a mud wall sown with phosphorescent eyes
a hand that draws the curtains
a child urinating at the end of a street
a funeral procession
a dog chasing after mirrors
a misanthropist fly
an insult lost in the night
a woman waking up and calling her son
an inexistent son
they are all objects ready to arouse desire
when the door opens the house is empty
in the church the rats listen to the litany
make the thirsty thirstier
make the hungry hungrier
oh, it's enough already, I have already touched the wing
I have already touched flight and cloud and rain
we can't proceed further
on the road of voluptuousness.

(1952)

THE TRUE PROPHET IN
THE FALSE LABYRINTH

An old soundless bell
locked inside the circle of gallops
four temptations
that coincide with the four cardinal points
impossible to conquer space
impossible to separate the light
from the resplendent face
in the confines of noise
certainty is waiting
this is the country which geographers call yesterday
the one explorers never conquered
in the edges of light
the woman surrenders
the woman sown with vegetal hallucinations
casting stones at solitude
the onanists slow down the growth of plants

The executioner who walks barefoot
is a woman of torturing perfection
the woman who lives invisibly
the one who sets off the way of darts.

By night
at the bottom of the stairs
the executioner woman empties out noise
and makes her perfect spasms ripple
irresistible temptation
of the four cardinal points of love.

(1957)

A SONG IN ONE HAND AND
DANGER IN THE OTHER

After the hands are separated
thousands of charred faces
thousands
the song of a solitary bird in a quiet morning
the masked men turn on the machines
man is singing in the antechambers of death.
Who is the one giving orders?
Who is it that sings after or before a quiet morning?
Who opens the doors of happiness? Who prepares the escape?
Sometimes a ferocious wind, sometimes a song,
a witness takes off the mask of fear
and confesses to being the author of the crimes
and the utensils roll down and halt their marching retinues
nothing is forbidden
                      the motorcyclist observes carefully
nothing stops
and then what
there are no answers there are no names for days that repeat
themselves
the innocent victims tremble on the stairs
the escape dies out the wheels wear themselves out
and all we are left with is the threat of vertigo the trace of emptiness
a man lost at the crossroads of accidents
and at the very moment that the hands sink,
into the room bursts
the song's complete uncertainty.

(1957)

ALL THE HEADS ARE COMBUSTIBLE

Excited by this statement the Pope opens the locks of his memory.
Governments tremble. Sagacious messages are exchanged. Repentant
seismologists pray for the age of catastrophes to begin. A museum of
images is dragged away by an overflowing river. Suddenly the most
beautiful image is bestowed the honors of the shipwreck. The unforeseen remains intact.

Intact yet besieged by the cold. Sub-zero temperatures freeze the furor
of a desperate crowd. The most beautiful image refuses the honors.
An inexplicable confusion spreads and invades the monasteries. The
churches reconcile while the martyrs get drunk. Suddenly the most
beautiful image is the violence in times of crisis. Dwarves take precautions.

The crowd sprouts. It spreads like an immortal pest. Bloody and
bloodthirsty. Angels of prey seize the properties of heaven. The
expected darkness comes. A merciless struggle makes friendship
intolerable. All means of communication are at a standstill. Splendid
processions cross the vertigo of night.

Similarly reality is torn to pieces. Cities come crashing down. Clouds
of ash compose this contorted world. An aberrant cleverness seeks to
grab on to anything. The merchant of surrender becomes the master of
his own destiny. The inexhaustible voraciousness of light dissolves the
solidity of objects. The spectators improve their blindness.

The last seismologists scrutinize with concern the tremors of our
obsessions. A solid fire is drowning at the center of the earth. An
unexpected tautness sets among drunkards who carefully avoid each
other. Senseless cruelty puts on an exciting show. Curiosity takes over
the cold that follows passion. Then the cold begins to burn and its fire
spreads to the tortured heads. Reality aquires the characteristics of an
unconfessed pain. The balloon vendors yield to fire. Casket builders
hesitate.

Meanwhile the serene heads are burning. The ideas crackle among the flames. The fire of intolerance lights the roads of this most marvelous of hatreds. The uneven fire of wounds stimulates good humor. The fire of pride mixes with the smoke of begging eyes. Love's invisible fire kindles cruelty. The cycle of creaking ashes comes to an end.

When the fire goes out the spectators die a natural death and great confusion follows time's battle against time. The inexistence of love is confirmed. The prelates smile enigmatically. An enormous amount of documentation has been collected but witnesses refuse to appear in court. The ants swarm inside a supernatural state of equality. The unbreathable air spreads over men and at last the earth belongs to the defeated.

(1967)

SUDDENLY IT IS SNOWING

Suddenly it is snowing.
When did the eyes turn into perpetual movement?
Breath of light you discover the night in things
a river is born at sundown
it drags the boats down the confines where anguish turns into waiting
a deceitful sun
     an endless
present stops the summer's acute pain
the avid sailor
     is discreetly killed
and in the blue distance
you give birth to a god that searches for death.

(1972-73)

I HAVE FOUND THE SECRET OF YOUR EYES

Look at me
I am searching for a golden cantharide at the bottom of the well
and in order to save the night I kill sleepwalkers.
Look at me until the sources stop flowing
and tremours are consumed
in the stillness of your eyes.
Is it because of the absence of hours
that you have stopped believing in the night?
Love is the way in which the rivers ripen
it is a vertiginous pastime at the edge of the abyss
and you have begun to walk the tightrope of my dreams
to adorn the death of my steps.

In order that your light alone may illuminate me
demand that today be the last day
demand the collapse of heights
extract white stains from the sun
strange eyes pass by

Look at me
look at me in the light of a universe without worlds
in the light of a ferocious dawn
look at me with your teeth
and through the spray
of endless oceans waiting for us.

(1952)

ONE MORE SHOW

The lady is overcome with cold
the lady is tired of everything
the lady does not know how to travel the shadows
the lady carries her knife on her chest
loudspeakers scare away the barefoot onlookers
the lady is sobbing as she thinks of her bleeding breast
the traveling orator
makes allusion to the sirens' song
the lady's tears fecundate the multitude's good mood
a very dignified individual hastily takes down notes
too many tears
the neon signs calmly take down notes
a breast, just one breast
cannot beat the calculation of probabilities
a good lady gets confused with the siren's song
with the song of life
she smiles
the orator has fulfilled his mission
the very dignified gentleman calms down
the neon signs are turned off
the show is over
the insatiable pupil remains motionless
behind the ones who leave.

(1952)

Alvaro Mutis

Colombia
1923

NOCTURNE

Tonight the rain is falling once again on the coffee trees.
The rain falls on the leaves of the plantain
on the tall branches of the *cambulo*,
tonight, persistent and vast waters pour down
and the ditches and the rivers swell,
they moan under the weight of the nocturnal load of vegetal mud.
The rain is beating down on the zinc roofs,
its presence sings, it keeps me away from sleep,
it leaves me stranded among restless growing waters
in this freshest of nights which drips
between the vaulted coffee branches
and slips away among the sickly trunks of the giant trees.
Suddenly, in the middle of this night,
the rain is falling once again on the coffee trees
and surrounded by the vegetal clamor of the waters,
the intact matter of days gone by comes back to me
divested of the immaterial labors of time.

(1961)

CAPTAIN COOK'S DEATH

When they asked him what Greece was like, he spoke of a long row of rest houses rising by the edge of a sea whose bitter waters washed the sharp stones of those narrow beaches in slow waves like oil.

When they asked him what France was like, he remembered a narrow corridor between two public offices where mean guards were registering a woman who smiled with shame, while the sound of the water splashing on the cables rose from the courtyard.

When they asked him what Rome was like, he uncovered a fresh scar on his groin which he claimed was from a wound he sustained while trying to break the window of a streetcar abandoned in the outskirts of the city, where women go to embalm their dead.

When they asked him whether he had seen the desert, he gave a detailed description of the erotic customs and the migratory calendar of the insects that nest in the porosity of the marble which the saltpeter of the bay and the incessant hands of the merchants who travel the coast have worn down.

When they asked him what Belgium was like, he spoke of the correlation between the weakening of desire when faced with a naked woman lying on her back, smiling awkwardly, and the intermittent and progressive rusting of certain firearms.

When they asked him about a port on the Strait, he showed them the dissected eye of a bird of prey inside which one could see the shadows of a song.

And when they asked him how far he had ventured, he answered that a freighter had dropped him off in Valparaiso where he took care of a blind woman who sang in the squares and claimed to have been dazzled by the light of the Annunciation.

(1961)

SONATA

Do you know what lies behind the steps of the harp and beckons from
    another time, from other days?
Why is it that a face, a gesture glimpsed from a train as it reaches its
    final destination,
before you become one with the city that slips away into mist and
    rain.
Why is it that they come back to visit you one day to utter through
    voiceless lips the word that could have saved you?
Look where you have set up camp! Why the anchor which stirs
    blindly in the deep? You do not know.
A great spread of water slowly rocks the vast domains offered to the
    afternoon sun,
waters of a great river which struggles against a sea that is cruel and
    cold, whose waves rise against the sky and then disappear into the
    muddy plains of the delta.

It may be so.
Those there may tell you something
or remain fiercely silent and you still will not know.
Do you remember the time she came down for breakfast and suddenly
    you saw her more child-like, more distant, more beautiful than
    ever?
Something was waiting for us in ambush there.
You knew it of course: A dull pain constricting the chest.
Someone spoke.
A servant dropped a dish.
Laughter at the next table,
something broke the rope that was pulling you out of a deep well,
    like Joseph and the merchants.
You spoke and the sadness you knew so well stayed with you,
and the bittersweet charm of her surprise at the world
rose in the air each day like a banner to signal your presence and the
    exact place of your battles.
Who are you, then? Where do those things about a port come from?
And, the theme the viola weaves
as it attempts to take you to a certain square, to the silent old park

with its pond where the joyful summer boats sail by?
Not everything can be known.
Not everything belongs to you.
Not this time, at least. You are learning to resign yourself,
to allow something else in you to finally sink to the bottom
and you are left more alone, a stranger,
like a waiter they shout at in the morning disorder of a hotel:
orders, insults, vague promises spoken in all the languages of the
world.

(1961)

MAQROLL'S PRAYER

> *"Tu as marché par les rues de chair?*
> *Babylone* — René Crevel

The prayer of Maqroll the Gaviero is not complete here. We have gathered only a few of its most salient sections and recommend to our friends that they be used on a daily basis as an efficacious antidote against incredulity and groundless happiness.

Maqroll the Gaviero said:

Lord, go after those who adore the soft snake!
Make everyone conceive of my body as the inexhaustible fountain of
   your infamy.
Lord, make the wells in the middle of the ocean dry up, there where
   the fish copulate without successfully achieving reproduction.
Wash the courtyards of all military headquarters and watch over the
   dark sins of the sentry. Allow, oh Lord, the ire of your words to
   rise in the horses as well as in merciless old women.
Make the dolls become disjointed.
Shed light in the bedroom of the clown, oh Lord!
Why do you inspire that immodest smile of pleasure in the sphinx
   made of rags preaching in waiting rooms?
Why do you take away from the blind man the cane he uses to tear at
   the dense felt with which desire surprises him in the dark?
Why do you prevent the jungle from entering the parks, from
   devouring the sand paths which the incestuous ones walk like
   straggling lovers in days of feast?
With your Assyrian beard, with your callous hands, oh fecund one,
   preside over the blessing of public swimming pools and the
   subsequent bathing of those adolescents who have not sinned!
Oh Lord, accept the pleas from this watchful supplicant and grant
   him the favor of dying wrapped in the dust of cities, of lying
   down on the steps of an infamous house lit by all the stars in the
   heavens.
Remember, Lord, that your serf has patiently observed the laws of
the herd. Do not forget his face. Amen.

(1953)   *Alvaro Mutis*   233

GAVIERO'S VISIT

For Gilberto Aceves Navarro

His appearance had completely changed. It was not as if he looked
older, worked over by the passing of time and the rage of the climates
he frequented. The time lapsed in his absence had not been that long.
It was something else. Something that his eyes betrayed, a lassitude.
Something about his shoulders, devoid now of expressive movement,
rigid as though they no longer had to bear the weight of life, the urge
of all its miseries. His muted voice was of a velvety and neutral tone.
It was the voice of someone who speaks because the silence of others
is unbearable to him.

He took the rocking chair to the corridor which faced the coffee
trees by the river's edge and sat down on it with the attitude of some-
one who is there to wait, as though the fast approaching evening
breeze could bring relief to his deep yet imprecise misfortune. The
faraway currents of the waters breaking against the large stones kept
company with his words, adding a certain opaque happiness to the
monotonous review of his affairs, like someone always immersed in
the same indifferent condition, forever defeated, a hostage of nothing.

"I sold women's clothes in the narrows of the *Guasimo* river. The
women from the valley who come down on special days and who must
cross the river on foot, always get their clothes wet despite their
efforts at gathering their skirts around their waists. Here and there
they would end up buying a few things from me in order not to go into
town looking like that.

"Years ago the sight of those dark skinned thighs, those round
buttocks and bellies firm like the chests of doves, would surely have
sent me into unbearable ravings. I was forced to abandon the place
when a jealous brother descended on me holding a machete in the air,
thinking that I was making advances on his sister, a young woman
with green eyes whom I was helping to try on a flowered percale
petticoat. She stopped him in time. Fed up, I sold off the rest of the
merchandise in a matter of hours, and left that place behind me, never
to return .

It was around this time that I made my home for a few months
inside a train car which had been left behind on some unfinished

tracks. I think I already spoke about that experience before. Besides, it matters little.

After, I traveled down to the coast and enlisted with a freighter that did cabotage in places full of mist and merciless cold. In order to pass the time and distract myself from the boredom, I would go down to the engine room to tell the stokers stories about the last four Dukes of Burgundy. I had to shout because of the deafening roar of the boiler. They always asked me to repeat the story of Fearless John at the hands of Orleans' men on the Montereau bridge, as well as the story of the wedding of Reckless Charles with Marguerite of York. I ended up doing nothing else during those endless crossings in the mist surrounded by huge blocks of ice. The captain forgot about me until one day, when the foreman went to him with the story that I was not letting the stokers do their work, that I was filling their heads with fables about the murder of important people, about unbelievable attempts on people's lives. He had caught me unawares as I was telling them the end met by the Duke of Nancy. Who knows what the poor man thought I was talking about. They let me off at a port of the Escalda river without any belongings other than my mended rags and an inventory of the anonymous burial grounds in the rocky cemeteries of San Lázaro.

Following that, I organized a fortnight of preaching and prayers at the entrance of the refinery in Río Mayor. I advertised the coming of a new Kingdom of God where there would be a strict, meticulous exchange of sins and penance, so that each hour of the day or the night might hold an inconceivable surprise, a joy as brief as it could be intense. I sold small leaflets with the litanies of a good death as well as a summary of the essential aspects of the doctrine. I have forgotten almost all of them, save that in my dreams I sometimes recall three of the invocations:

> *trail of life let your scale free*
> *eye of water gather your shadows*
> *angel of mud cut off your wings*

I often wonder whether in fact those sentences form part of the original litany, or whether they are born of some of my more mournful recurrent dreams. It is too late to find out, and besides, it is not something that interests me a great deal.

All of a sudden, Gaviero interrupted the relation of his increasingly precarious wanderings and threw himself into a long monologue at once disjointed and without apparent purpose, but which I remember with painful fidelity and a vague boredom of imprecise origin. He continued:

"Because in the end, all these occupations, meetings and places have ceased being the true substance of my life. So much so that I no longer know which were born of my imagination and which belong to real experience. Thanks to them and through them, I try in vain to flee some of my obsessions, the real and permanent ones which make up this final fabric, the obvious destiny of my wanderings in the world. It is not easy to isolate them or call them by name, but they go more or less like this:

"To negotiate a happiness similar to the one experienced on certain days of my childhood in exchange for the complaisant brevity of life.

"To prolong solitude without being afraid of encountering who we really are. To engage in dialogue with someone who remains hidden in order not to sink us into a horror without exit.

To know that no one listens to anyone. That no one knows anything about anyone. That the word in itself is deceitful, a trap that covers, conceals and buries the construction of our dreams and our truths, all of which are marked by the sign of the incommunicable.

"To learn above all, not to trust one's memory. What we think we remember is completely foreign and different from what really happened. Those irritating moments of sorry boredom which years later memory brings back as the episodes of a splendid happiness, are too numerous. Nostalgia is the lie thanks to which we get closer to death. To live without remembering could perhaps be the secret of the gods.

"When I talk about my roaming, my foolish ravings and my secret orgies, I do so only to suppress two or three beastly screams, heart-rending cavern-like cries which would be the most efficient way of saying what I truly feel and what I am. However, I am getting lost in these digressions and that is not why I am here.

His eyes aquired a fixity of lead as though they were trapped inside a thick wall of colossal dimensions. His lower lip trembled lightly. He crossed his arms over his chest and began to rock slowly, as though he wished the rocking to echo the murmur of the river. The smell of fresh mud, crushed plants and decaying sap signaled to us that the tide was rising.

Gaviero remained silent for a long time until the night fell on us with the vertiginous darkness typical of the tropics. Fearless glow worms were dancing in the warm silence of the coffee trees. He began to speak again and got lost in another digression whose meaning I began to lose as he delved deeper into the darker zones of himself. All of a sudden, he started to once more to bring up facts about his past. I picked up the thread of his monologue:

"I have had few surprises in my life — he said— and none of them deserves to be told, yet to me, each one rings out the mournful energy of the bell of catastrophe. One morning while I dressed surrounded by the burning drowsiness of a river port, I found myself in the ramshackle cubicle of a miserable brothel. There was a photograph of my father hanging on the wooden wall. The picture showed him sitting on a wicker rocking chair in the lobby of a white hotel in the Caribbean. My mother had kept it on her night table and it had remained in the same spot all through her long widowhood. —Who is it? — , I asked the woman I had spent the night with and whom until now I had only seen in the unkempt disorder of her flesh and her beastly features. — It's my father— she answered with a smile which betrayed a toothless mouth, all the while covering her obese nakedness with a sheet wet with sweat and misery. — I never met him, but my mother, who also used to work here, always spoke about him and kept some of his letters as though they could keep her forever young —. I finished putting on my clothes and walked out into the wide, unpaved street, into the piercing sun and the racket of radios, cutlery and dishes which rose from the cafés and the bars now beginning to fill up with a regular clientele of drivers, cattle farmers and soldiers from the air base. I thought with dismay that this was precisely the corner of my life I should never have turned. Too bad.

"On another occasion, I ended up in a hospital in Amazonia in order to get cured from an attack of malaria which was sapping my strength and kept me in a constant state of delirium. Even though the heat was unbearable during the night, it kept me away from the whirlwind of vertigo in which a foolish phrase or the tone of voice impossible for me to identify were the center around which my fever turned and which made my bones ache. Next to me, a businessman who had been bitten by the *pudridora* spider, kept fanning the black pustule which had invaded the whole of his left side. —It will soon dry up — he commented in a cheerful voice —it will soon be dry and I will leave and close down the operation. I will be so rich. I will never again remember this hospital bed, nor this goddamned jungle good only for monkeys and alligators —. The matter at hand seemed to consist of a complicated exchange system of spare parts for the hydroplanes which linked up the region. This was done through preferential import licenses controlled by the army which were free of custom duties and taxes. At least that is what I awkwardly remember now, because the man would spend the whole night talking about the most insignificant details of the business, and one by one these began to blend themselves into the maelstrom of my malaria crisis. At dawn, I would finally succeed in falling asleep, but always feeling fenced in by the pain and fear which had kept me company until well into the night. —Look, here are the papers. They'll all go to hell. You'll see. I'm out of here tomorrow, without fail — he said to me. He kept repeating himself with ferocious insistence while he brandished a bunch of blue and pink papers filled with stamps and inscriptions written in three languages. The last thing I heard him say before I fell into a long feverish trance was: — Oh what a nice rest! What joy! This whole damn thing is over and done with! —I woke up with the din of a gunshot which sounded as if the end of the world had arrived. I turned to look at my neighbor: his head, blown apart by the bullet still trembled with the spongy consistency of a rotting fruit. I was transferred into another room and that is where I lay between life and death until the rainy season arrived and with the breeze new life was granted me.

"I don't know why I am telling you all these things. In truth I came here to leave these papers with you. It's up to you to do with them as you wish in case we don't meet again. There are some letters from my youth, some pawning receipts and the drafts of the book I will not be finishing. It deals with the secret motives that drove Cesar Borgia, Duke of Valentinois, to go to the court of his brother-in-law, the King of Navarre, in order to pledge his support against the King of Aragon, and how he died in an ambush set by soldiers one early morning in the outskirts of Viana. The story meanders through dark zones which years ago, I believed were worthy of being brought to light. I am also leaving you an iron cross which I found in an ossuary in Almogávares in the garden of an abandoned mosque in the outskirts of Anatolia. It has always brought me luck but I think the time has come for me to part with it. I am leaving with you the bills and receipts, proof of my innocence concerning the explosives factory which I owned at the mines of El Sereno. The profit was to allow me and the Hungarian medium who was then my partner, as well as a Paraguayan associate, to retire on the island of Madeira. They fled with everything and the responsibility of dealing with the bills fell on my shoulders. The matter was annulled years ago, but an urge to keep things in order has forced me to keep these receipts which I no longer want to carry with me.

"Well, I will now say good-bye. I am taking an empty barge down to Ciénaga del Mártir and if I find a few passengers downstream I will make a bit of money to keep me going."

He got up and extended his hand with a gesture at once ceremonious and military, so characteristic of him. Before I could insist that he spend the night and that he begin his descent down river the next morning, he disappeared among the coffee trees whistling that old and fairly dated song which had so enchanted us when we were young. I was left behind going over his papers. There I found a number of traces of Gaviero's life which he had never mentioned before. I was in the middle of that, when I heard rising from below the thunder of his steps on the bridge across the river, followed by their echo on the zinc roof which covers it. I felt his absence and began to remember his voice and his gestures whose evident change I had perceived earlier and which now came back to me like a fateful warning telling me that I would never see him again.

(1984)

A WORD

When suddenly, in the middle of one's life a word appears which had
  never been uttered before
a dense tide welcomes us and the great voyage begins in this newly
  initiated magic
which rises like a scream in an immense abandoned hangar where
  the moss covers the walls.
Surrounded by the rust of forgotten beings who inhabit a ruined
  world, a word suffices,
a word and the unhurried dance begins and leads us through the   thick
  dust of cities,
from the stained-glass window of a dark rest house, to courtyards
  where the soot flowers and dense shadows make their nests,
damp shadows which give life to tired women.
No truth can inhabit those corners. A mute fear surprises us
  filling life with its vinegar breath, a rancid vinegar flowing down
  the wet pantry of a humble brothel.
And that is not all.
There is the conquest of warm regions where insects watch the
  mating of the guardians of the crop
who grow hoarse in those endless plantations of sugar cane cleaved
  by fast flowing waters
and opaque reptiles with rich, white skin.
Oh, the insomnia of the watchmen who beat tirelessly on the sonorous
  oil drums
in order to frighten away the diligent insects which the night sends
  away like a promise of wakefulness!
On the way to the sea, those things are soon forgotten.
When a woman is waiting with her white abundant thighs open like
  the branches of a centenary *písamo* tree in bloom,
the poem reaches the end and there is no longer any point to its
  monotonous threnody
which rises from the murky yet always renewed source flowing
  through the tired bodies of obsessed gymnasts.

Just one word.
One word and the dance
of fertile misery begins.

(1953)

FIVE IMAGES

1

Autumn is the preferred season of the converted. Behind the orange mantle of the leaves, under the gold bored by invisible worms the messengers of winter and forgetting, it is easier to survive the new duties that overwhelm the newcomers to a fresh theology. One must doubt the serenity with which the leaves wait for their inevitable fall, their vocation of dust and nothingness. They will remain a little longer in order to witness the inexorable condition of time: the final defeat of the loftiest destinies of freshness, of ripeness.

2

There are objects which never travel. This is how they remain immune to forgetting and to the more arduous tasks imposed by use and by time. They stop in an eternity made of parallel instants woven by nothingness and habit. This particular condition places them on the margins of the tide and life's fevers. Neither doubt nor horror visit them and the vegetation watching over them is just a tenuous trace of their vain continuance.

3

The dreams that insects dream are made of unfamiliar metals which pierce like thin drills into the stone's darkest kingdom. No one should raise his hand to touch the tiny stars that are born during the after-noon rest with a sustained chafing of elytra. The dreams that insects dream are made of metals known to the night only through great silent feasts. Careful. A bird descends and behind it descends the morning to set up its tents, tall canvases of the day.

4

No one invited this character in order that he recite his part from a stage which they raise elsewhere, like a scaffold for the innocent. Neither his obsequious bowing, nor the false modesty of his features which reveal that he is a tattletale, will win him favor. The murderers are searching for him in order to drown him in a bath of mint and liquid lead. His hour is coming despite his stealthy steps and an air which seems to say: "here I am worth nothing."

5

It is at the bottom of the sea that slow ceremonies take place. They are presided over by the stillness of matter which millions of years ago the earth relegated to the forgetting of the depths. The calcareous cuirass once knew the sun and the dense alcohols of dawn. This is why it reigns in its stillness with the certainty of forget-me-nots. It flowers in fainting gestures when the medusas wake up. It is as though life were inaugurating the earth's new face.

(1982)

Eduardo Anguita

Chile

1914-1992

FINAL PASSING

The door may open,
the dog's barking may come in:
we need know nothing.

As long as the wind does not invade us
and our eyes can find their way among the furnishings
of diversity inside the fears of each dead man,
we can laugh inside this foamy darkness.

The certainty of the one who opens his private suit
leaving the white traces of his ravings for all to see.
Just a little force and one can make a concentrate from invisible ash,
shadows, my private death.

Stones in the eyes: silence has turned to solid,
solitary hands are stepping over the body.
This is how we love the statue's air,
the very air that urges us unto old age.

The man walks into a room a like this one
and dons the suit that will guide him, forever.

(1934)

THE POLYHEDRON AND THE SEA

I was given a polyhedron as I stood by the sea,
a solid yet invisible body,
a compact gathering of distances,
with its hardened silences,
its neighbouring absence:
the more palpable it became, the more forsaken.

How sweet to let myself slip along its edges,
faster than eyes turning toward the sun,
blind flight along a pristine line leading me to the encounter.
When I wanted to think about where I was, vertigo overcame me:
Edge. Line. Nothing.
I slid along the nothingness that the two faces of the polyhedron
    formed when they kissed.
From the lineal kiss I wanted to rise to the lip,
lie down on those surfaces, finally rest on the golden extension.
And while doing so, I forgot about the deep blue of the ocean
my valley of ghostly quartz.

What was this? The extension was pure limit :
as one volume was being born, another one was dying!
In the cutting silence, the knife-edge grew narrower than a line
    drawn between kiss and mouth,
Did I believe I was touching substance?
Just volume against volume unrobing,
unattainable and fleeting, nothingness was drawing me in with
    its absent love!
Standing before the ocean I shouted:
''Everything is distance!''

What do you know? A hundred ten-year-old children,
do they add up to one hundred centuries?

I do not know. I threw the polyhedron back into the sea:
I understood that it had lied to me.

II

When wine's kiss informs the lip, do you know what you know?
They gather there, in the wine. They come from distant places.
There is taste and color, smell and many more things,
weight that is soft, darkness made flame,
they come together like a simple example.
But this is not the wine.

On the other hand, behind the water's soft caress, ready to disappear
    when you wish to grasp it,
lies not moisture, not freshness which soaks and drenches,
but something else! Water too serves as example!

You are looking at a black and white etching and like a child,
you turn it around to see whether the street continues on the back,
whether the back of the picture will show the little girl's nape.
Were you crying when you looked?
You did not understand.
It is just an illusion to help you while you wait.
We see the world, its avenues, a deep living mouth, warmth,
    softness and consistency.
The sea we gaze at is concentrated and vast and moves,
    remains fixed:
who could have expressed it so clearly through an etching!
The sun's face — still invisible to us — is not the sun,
but a space where the sun will be.
Summer's smell is the shadow of smell.
The taste of peach, mere shadow of taste!

Numbers as they relate to the taste of things that enumerate.
They would have you believe that what counts is the relationship
    between one note and another.
But no! Hear the resounding timbre of the bassoon or the oboe,
the black brilliance of the tuba.
Viola, your substantial wines welcome the sun into your human
    branches,
warm angel in the ear of honey, in the veins of the fruit,
summer's blood and the golden bee crowning

the rope of the joyous life I am about to hear.
This is what awaits you: not the line on the water, but water itself.

And what you are drinking now
is the water's line, its number.
The broken column lies motionless,
like a game of distances
embraced, adored only as long
as they remain respectfully contained.
Will you love distance? Will you love volume, form?
Oh, but the column stands as another example. It is not here.
It is simply a place, an instant.
Volume. Time. Heaviness.
Form and distance will return,
here they will touch and close up, resist.
But none can unfold into plenitude.
And the column, is it not abstinence?
Is it not a pause? A corner? A compromise?
Silence?

Tell me: what does freshness have that water doesn't have?
What does a liquid have that is not water?
Yet water, is much, much more than either,
so much more than what is ductile and liquid and curved.
And, is it not true that you care more for water than for fluidity,
for what is curved and liquid?

I know that there is something you prefer over and above water.
I do not know what it is. I only know that it is a shadow of the other.
What you see in a puddle of water is the reflection of water.
And this water which I drink
is nothing more than a hollow corner reserved for water!

III

(Priest): Brothers, think of this life as a mere passage. This life is but a simulacrum. Whatever you may think you will find, is illusory. Do not fool yourselves. Do not cling to worldly goods. Yearn for the things of this world only in the measure in which they serve you as instruments, as an explanation for the other life.

Behold:
The flowers have no color,
The sea is white,
Music is white,
The air is empty,
Dawn has not come.
The fruit is weightless.
And still I do not exist.
Inside every voice there is a great hollow.
What covers it? A sheath of gold?
A promise maintains this situation:
Space is a just a reserve.
Oh, the world is two distant lips.
My brothers: the world is not a kiss!

"Why is it so?", you may ask. Why this life, imperfect and deceitful? Why, "vanity of vanities," as the Preacher said?

We have brought about this great wound.
The world is an ulcer: there is no substance.
Mercy has allowed the orbit to exist.
I come from being.
Now I come from non-being.
Surprise yourself with what is here and what is not
here.
The cracks in the porcelain are beautiful,
But so are the grooves in the milling machine
And if space were open, there would just be emptiness.
They would not be possible.
If space were closed like a compact substance,
Where would the rose open? Where would we open?

We do not become larger.
They are digging into us!

I invite you to meditate about the fallacy of our ephemeral existence,
about this diminished world, about this matter porous like a sponge,
this flesh eaten away by time. And I invite you to ponder the truth of
the other. Let us by means of this painful yet hopeful example, com-
pare the inconsistency of matter with the eternity of the spirit.

> The eyes are an illusion. What they see is true.
> The kiss is solid. Lips are steam.
> Tears are soft. Crying is hard.
> The hand is a cloud. It falls with each caress.
> What is real is not the voice, but the word.
> The object disappears. The name remains.
> You are not here. I am not here
> When will we be?
> And the promise is already made:
> "I am the Way, the Truth.
> I am Life."
> Yes brothers: for Him.
> We will get there someday
> Someday we will be,
> Someday we will live.
> Amen.

IV

I threw the polyhedron back into the sea
and the arrogant sea dragged it away.

But, who are you?
Your miserly waves, your furious rags,
those deserted rooms where the light goes out,
what are they? They are so unreal and you shake them again
and again, hoping to expel their motionless hollowness.
Your transparent cones are threads turned inside out
where a blind man becomes thinner.

The prairies that you sow with salt and sound
are just mirrors of alternating emptiness.
Time breaks into drops, never to become joined again,
it shuts out the sea with each damned instant.
Your abyss is lonelier, more deprived than the hard planes
of the deceitful polyhedron which you would rather scorn.

The instantaneous bell is ringing in solitude
and when your multitudes, when your absent waters
roll over the ephemeral edges of the waves
everything ceases to exist except a vast
quivering fright made blue by unattainable infinity.
Vanity of vanities, you, the sea!

Suspension of hollow threads quickly warping,
salt that sews and sews
nothing.
Slices of orbits, spaces without substance, without hollowed eyes,
pure profile: you can't fool me!
Your crowns, your tongues, your convulsed sparkles,
they are the wounds of an infinite, tormented distance.
Your frenzied edges, your delirious acts of immodesty,
what are they? Thinned-out lines!
And what chokes is not the water, it is emptiness
lurking inside you drop after drop
wave after wave.
(The line swims on and on, it conjugates incessantly
the indefatigable word which no one utters).

Why do you convulse with wrath?
Do you not understand?
The kiss is firm. Lips are made of steam.
The hand is a cloud. It dies with each caress.
Tears are soft. Crying is hard.
The air is thin. The days are solid!

There are nights when we think we can hear you crying,
there are days when we think we can hear you laugh.
Illusion! Laughter and crying wander over you
like a misty idea unable to settle

on the face of a madman.
Your tears can't join this weeping,
your teeth do not touch laughter:
Oh, unfinished sea!

I want to cross the Acheron with you
—sea transported over different waters—
Face without a face, let us go!
The burning hollow of the sun
is waiting for the sun.
Do not fear: we are the guilty ones.
Two distant lips make up the world,
But no one has ever kissed!
Image of man, deserted image,
sea, like me, you possess nothing
Where are you, roaring nothingness?
Sea: we need you!

I am like you: uninhabited space.
I am like you: a terrible lesion.
You are like me: mad distances.
You are like me, with one half on the other side,
and music is possible with your empty staff.
You and me. Will we finally be?
Will we recover the True Face?
Will we recapture the Reality we lost?

Yes, I promise you.
But we will not return!

(1952)

VISIT

Wait for us under the plum tree, shepherd boy of the dead.
Open up that pond for us, the silent yard cleansed by the undertow of
    stars and by the sunset day after day.
Tall grasses bring only perfunctory silence to the wilting tomb stones.
Ancient messages to be read very slowly
Words not to be uttered,
But caressed softly by the warmth of the sun.
The unhurried lizard, the spider, the grasshopper, they pass
And the wind which blows from the barren plains of the sea calms
    down over them.
A great mirror stretches out over this solitude.

Open up, let us into the garden visited only
By those who are truly alive.
The hill that is born and dies at the foot of this chapel,
The petrified wave next to enemy rock: they are now forgiven,
They neither love nor hate each other, but are past.
Bones reached the bone, blood touched the pure flowing waters
And time has returned to time. Hill of the dead,
Eroded, augmented and purified by an invisible current.

End of summer. Little sense in saying it at the Totoral cemetery!
A garden where the years ripen better than summers in other orchards.
End of summer in this rural corner. Those who were always meant to
    live together have gathered here.
Eternity was here, next to them, behind the mud wall, behind the
    rustic wall built by Christian, the town's shepherd;
There, behind the house where friends were supposed to gather and
    tell one another the family news.
A place reserved for each one of them — outsiders in front of the
    house, outsiders in the vestibule,
Chatting, joking, shrill good-byes. But in the back, in the back,
The fragrant little orchard the owners always preferred when wilted
    because what is wilted is a sign of old, loyal friendship.
At the back of the house, on the other side of the fence,
An intimate conversation between eternal friends.

End of summer in this seaside cemetery.
First fall afternoon, golden sun, distant from the light,
Yet close because of its softness,
Go, slip over the hillside, fenced-in like an orchard.
Suspended tombs (the oars were left behind for the living, for
    the young, for the outsiders).
Among the blades of the alfalfa, the vain faded marble in rural
    eternity,
One can read the breath of the autumn sun:
    "Died on the 11th of May, 1857.
    Will soon be joined by
    Her inconsolable husband."
Oh, impatient youth: you etched on this gravestone the promise of
    reuniting *soon*. Soon.
Soon took so long in coming. It got waylaid, brought pain with it,
    lay hidden and was almost forgotten, but then it germinated,
    reappeared,

Matured: interminable years.

Now, next to her at last, as though they had always belonged together,
    like the quiet veins
    of marble, once a storm

Finally by her side!
    "He came here to join his
    Beloved wife
    January 6, 1902."
1857... 1902. Such a long time — 45 years — separating them...
And a long time — 48 years — since that other, unfortunate time,
    ceased to be,
So much time passed since their joyful reunion and our present
And so long — 93 years — between her death, when it all began and
    this time.
So much bitter time succeeding itself and stopping finally becoming
    happiness:
But the joyful time gone by was slowly forgotten and became unreal!
And, once again, from the other side of the fence as if everything had
    always been
    the past, made to our measure, to say:

It is good. It is real.
And how much more time yet until someone reads these pages
   so much later.
   Who, who can wait?
And the same sun kisses the hill, the suspended tombs. And...
End of summer.

We are in 1950 in a wilting orchard in Totoral, the hill covered with
   ivy and the dead.
The hill of friends. 1950! So much time wasted here where
   we came without thinking, crowding like a gust of
   children around a serious speaker.
Feverish veins, impetuous tears: Yes, they existed! They exist!
They *are*: traces on the marble, motionless like the sea when
   seen from above: an epitaph.
All this rescued through us who have suffered nothing, we who have
   been given the strangeness of the wind.

That long and distant *soon*,
For us, too eager, it is *soon* once again!

Both lives, both deaths, the two here next to each other, not even a
   weed grows between them.
Wife and husband face to face.
Time cloven, the wound should have healed
(Waters that a fleeting hand separated for a brief instant -45 years),
The word is now reunited,
And time is placid, lucid, admirable.
Wife and husband, two empty extremes
Bringing life to separation.
Together here, two lips
Of time forming one ancient
Nuptial kiss.

(1950)

ILLUMINATION OF GUERNICA

Fearsome night, rise to my tongue that I may drink you and
  transform you.
Night, loved and suffocated by a sun thick with twisted dust.
Blind animal, lower half, never static: sing your silvery demon,
Rise from the waters of the spirit, never lose your strength, never
  confuse yourself with deceitful clearness.
Spring forth from that closed background where authentic self-
  reflection is boiling.
May peace never render you impure, may it never be with you,
  nor with me, nor with you, my brothers.

Wisdom's face, its negligent fireworks
Lie outside wilting under their gray heaviness
Without surrendering, I see no better torture at the bottom of this
  ocean
Than modern architecture with its economical whiteness:
It will never understand Guernica.

Guernica: the sea, the sea. Someone with flagrant breasts is running
  inside this illusory phosphorescence
Guernica: someone saw it die, saw it come alive in the Passion
  according to St. John
Theological champagne: where is the crying? What academic
  conclusions claim to shed light on you, to know the outside of you?
In the center the innocent bull palpitates like an undying vegetable.
After the coming,
After the descent, or the ascent
The bull *exists* and the word it utters is a moan: *my God*
Do you hear the deafening tenderness of the animal that lives alone
  among the herds?
Listen to the sacred pendulum that excludes.
Listen, live this marble born again through the eyes,
  through tremors,
Listen to Prince Myshkin crying over the waters.

The desire to go back to the bonfire,
To be with the living trees, surrounded by the solitude of movable
    numbers
To be frightening like the roar that a virgin makes in the desert
    while still a virgin.
Flee, flee all you fearful animals
Eternal soul: Does the tongue betray the proximity of a monster?
Eternal sands, give me back my drop of blood

Do you wish to know which are the birds that fly close to the sea?
Are you blind? You will be pulled to pieces
Grab onto your bones even if they are the cold, freakish creatures
    of our mind's vanity

You will be free of your vestments
More available for the holocaust
You will die in the whirlwind of life, of God, of justice
Touch, forsaken, gnawing horns.
Tenderness penetrates insolence,
The living coal of essential sugars

Motionless, frank, desolate, instantaneous,
Transparent in its final reason for being,
The beast shines when it remembers its roots
While death requests its moons through the laws of grace.

(1937)

VENUS IN THE GARBAGE DUMP
(2 fragments)

When we lie down and the arms and the thighs of one are bound to
    those of the other:
This embrace is called
mixture of sesame seeds and rice.
When she, while recumbent, places one of her legs on my shoulder,
extends the other one and places that one over her shoulder
stretching out the first leg, quickly and alternately,
this is called the groove in the bamboo.

Oh body that is never truly possessed!
Bodies that dare not touch the mystery of the body!

Mouth to mouth, breast to breast,
part to part, whole to whole.
Later, also part to the whole.
To allude, to elude,
My hand could not stop dividing her, joining her in fluctuating
    meetings.
My palms, sensitive inner mirrors,
slid down her side to the accession juncture,
while her back and I fell in love

I did a half circle turn and my conscience was left
facing her feet, she on her back and I face down, one on top of the
    other:
This is how we did what I call
sincerely
the clepsydra.

I do not know which compartment was receiving, which was giving.
Even though we were naked, the inversion of our bodies became
    necessary
in order to empty all the sand and be left truly innate.
She and I: past and future,
one consummated, the other consumed.
Midnight, no doubt.

Challenge me with your thighs,
may your previous wound tremble.
I will go in deep, deep
so we may become more confused in each other
than a fact within the time it occupies.
I enter, my young one, my warmth, I enter you,
as weeping enters weeping.
Stars run along syllables
softer than animals.

The horror when I am inside you, woman, like a key gone mad inside
velocity.

Your breasts, pain's heads
exist under a sky I would gladly devour
mixed with the waters of my body.

Your new wounds travel me like a mother making her way
in the fire.

When a woman receives a man, her eyes
resemble an endless step which is never taken,
and the space between her eyebrows is a bridge over pleasure,
over this river,
so I may measure my reach, my agony
and my consummation.

....

Even the most rustic of men seeks to possess Beauty.
When the large brute takes the woman by the waist,
his hand does not stay there:
he moves it down to her hip.
But his hand does not remain there:
it goes back to her waist,
admires, caresses hip
and waist in successive
quick movements
longing to embrace both,

longing to apprehend not one, not the other,
but their shared golden proportions.
5 is to 8 and the two are enhanced.
Seduced, exasperated, we do not succeed
in making our relationship a harmonious one.
You think that you yearn for the body:
Worm, you yearn for numbers!

Let us love furiously, let us hate vehemently:
5 is to 8, 5 is to 8... faster, faster,
let us make music and madness.
I dance you, golden section!

Can I possess? Will you destroy?

We who are hungry, will wander tonight
among sweet, unreachable numbers.

Because, there is no greater solitude than man's solitude
   before Beauty!

(The Worm):
—In Tenochtitlan the face remained hidden
from death, through masks made of other masks.
Buccal leopard masks
covered with frontal masks
and snake faces, and the snake
hidden and crowned by the eagle.
Never before had man's name
gone naked into battle:
bird and beast.
I broke my teeth in Tenochtitlan
with that changing cloud of masks.
Worm and death, we were fooled
by a warrior whose face was kept hidden
like the woman who does not surrender
every time she refuses to surrender her image and her name.
If I do not know what it is I am devouring, I do not devour:
one does not devour the unknown.

Deceitful wave, each passing instant changes you,
and I kiss mistakes on your lips made of spray.
Fierce betrayal, irrepressible ash,
what became of the dust worn down by love?
Man lives the instant alone
through the lies that mark the boundaries of his body.
Love, beauty, life, the word,
never undone, never captured.
The same sun bemoans probability,
another sun imagines what is past.
Impossible death, unattainable life:
worm and man: we were both deceived!

Whom did I love? Was it you, but somewhere else?
Or was it another woman, but here?
The woman I am kissing now,
is it the same person, but in a different place?
In a different time, is she the same person?
In a different time, does she remain the same?

The four of us can never be united!

A kilo of cotton does not weigh what a kilo of steel weighs.
You exemplify uniqueness.
You expel yourself. To repeat you is the other.
Your portrait of twenty years ago is strange!
What one feels once again,
dies for the first time.

In 1940 I thought: "In 1950 I will remember this year."
It is 1960 now and I remember that
in 1950 I remembered thinking that in 1940
I decided that in 1950
I would remember 1940.

Fatal. It is 1960. We predicted this years ago!
The nightingale sings. Let's repeat three times:
Tsew, tsew, tsew.
"What time is it?" *Tsew, tsew, tsew.*

What instant are you living in, bird of the forest?
Solitary hedges, fresh smell of the leaves.
The immemorial sound of the sea.
Tsew — one whistle levels off the new and the ancient;
child and old man are the same age:
an instant, an instant, an instant.

When a woman is with a man
and places her thoughts on another man not yet known to her,
and together or alternately lives out the moment,
while presuming the end of her current passion:
I accuse her of
divortium aquarum.

Beloved, beloved now. Besotted.
Coming, come in.
Lover, love over,
kiss me later .
Tell me while you face the other way:
Love, I will wait for you yesterday.

(1960)

Humberto Díaz-Casanueva

Chile

1907-1992

THE VISION

I lay darkly with my eyelids cast toward horror
perhaps at the end of the world, my sleepless hands placed
between the wind that blew through me and the rubble of the sky.
No ideas came to me then. In an immense whiteness
my temples got lost like crowns drained of their blood
and my bones glowed like sacred bronzes.
These translucent hands and the sea in magic order,
touched the summit from which dawn softly flows.
The purest road, light turned to solid by sleeping waters
as I flowed back to my origins, breaking
my white skin. Only its oils gleamed.
My morning arrived in this world born of the earth
perhaps from a sky long since waiting, whose shadow step
was silenced by my ear ringing like the wind's nest.
I was lucid for the first time but not with my tongue or its echoes,
without tears to show me options and golden melodies.
I let free a dove and it closed my blood inside silence.
I understood that the brow was formed over a vast dream
like a slow scab on a wound that bleeds without ceasing.
That was all. The night was turning my arms into secret branches
my back was probably settling into its own shadow.
I turned to darkness, to the larvae pressed against my forehead again
and a great fear made me rejoice in my heart with its clear songs.
I am certain that I have touched the ashes of my own death,
ashes that are my deepest sleeplessness when I dream.

(1931)

264

RIVER OF LIFE

When nuptial winds lift her solar breasts
a kiss holds the white-skinned star inside her.
For love, her body becomes death's softest pause,
her milk dissolves her purest layers for man.

An infant, the child of her abyss searches out the living clay
searches a feverish brow for dreams' dark hordes to rest on,
prisons for the heart overwhelmed by gods
because this being still owns the secret which precedes the soul.

The mother feels one of her veins, the two loose eyes floating there
unable perhaps to fix their invisible stamens, feels the feet
tapping inside her, asking her to show them the way of the earth:
She feels them now treading their own road while she sleeps.

While the mother naps, the child whispers his name to her,
begs her to assuage his fears of approaching the world,
because he is alive: destiny has tied the knots of her soul
and his memory is beginning to forget his true origins.

(1931)

BLIND PASSAGE

The prudent soul keeps itself from eyes consumed,
its cisterns bellow, drunk within,
fire refuses the wave with its vast creations
made golden by the solstice the soul soars
and its secret roots suit every shadow.
Immolated in my own laws, I am inside.
Oh, my uninhabited bee! Once the pristine breast is exhausted,
its honey no longer revives the empty torches.
I left the frightful world behind on mortal feet,
and here, between my wings, song is my purest luck.
But the light does not suffice for the corn's ear and the poem
does not need dazzling form or potency
to turn angels into song, to turn wind into star.
The maritime part of my body irritates the horizon
black bones sustain me as does the devouring prisoner in me,
marbles and doves settle in my weeping.
This porous brow is motionless under vain silences,
swift smokes change the direction of my song
quickly, like a head in death.
I am the tremulous half of things underneath me
which my whole being assumes over sudden flames.
Under furious stars, someone attracts them mercilessly:
they are too numerous for this place: here only dreams can graze.
The herds are closing in on my defending nation.
The wakeful mind is insufficient for its shepherd,
so I follow my infinite hostage gods:
under their weight my arrow is starting to breathe death.

(1931)

THE PILLAR OF SALT
Canto II (fragments)

I

Come, living ones at the altar, hold me! Come now, may your
    chaste presence dispel the cloud at my feet.
You say, *"It is nothing."* And the singing grass begins to cover the
    cesspool
"It is nothing, it is nothing." I repeat. A bell tolls inside my nestling
    heart.
Come, come and shelter me from this mouth, clamoring for words
    like a dispute between signals,
Shelter me from my steps which an invisible needle is weaving.
Do not hesitate, oh living ones! My hearing is a fluttering of wings
    sustained by hurled silences.
When I come home at night they embrace me in the dark,
Their arms are a pit, their brows a fallen nest.
The sea throws my senses around like broken anchors,
The world disappears in a tremor, the street curls up like the tails of
    uncontrolled fogs.
I feel nothingness surround me. I am nothing, nothing, nothing. I am
    endless questioning, negations.
              the jolts of my own death,
              a detached shadow.
But I still am Me.
I am as though suspended, clinging to a vertiginous swing with my
    hands
I come back to my house and the hairy dog has been let loose, its
    spots are shiny eyes,
Devouring my threshold it howls as though I were a vagabond.
But the children embrace me like always. Yes, the children throw light
    on me, they bear witness!
"Oh, it is nothing children -I tell them- *I found this frozen doll. It
    fell from a giant window that gives onto the world:*
              Throw it into the fire!
And tell your mother that I want a cup of tea trimmed with kisses!"*

III

Tell me, oh living ones! Why does this great inherited spear hang
    from the middle of the lament,
From the dusty ceiling above our heads?
We feel it thrusting into us while we dream
And we drink its salty kiss
And pain ties our hands to the tree
And the song is a broken wave without space
Man devoured by thunder
Dragged far away
As he counts the days.
Come and give me shelter, oh living ones! Death, newly born, is
    shaking in my arms,
Stretching and shaking with fear like an unborn child.
It blinks unceasingly.
I feel it to be the sacred measure,
The precisely cut tunic.
Do I assign to it my accomplishments, gains and losses?
I confess that I have unknowingly prepared myself for death,
Death growing longer behind dream,
And I would have contained it between necklaces without ever
    letting go.
The beautiful young woman wrapped me in her thick hair, we slept,
Her avid breasts were covered in gold,
Her kissing was flowering tongue.
Pressed one against the other on her bosom:
This was life's dream.

V

I was a thinker among the mutterings of marine birds,
Hanging from a rock on a dark street,
Never waking and dying alive
Turning my ear inward to hear the bursting of faded tombstones.
Like the solitary man whose skin is stained, the flaming torch of day
Scorched my back

And I fled without glory into my blackened heart
Toward a mountain watched over by slingers.
I spent my years soaring with the eagle
And the higher the eagle soared, the longer the shadow it cast
Over my sleepless house.
I have climbed up the hill of this eternal, silent life so often,
Devouring a book marked by the autumn's charred leaf,
The bees danced on the breath of the dead, my thoughts
Were treading wax
My eyes were the curb of a well, my lips pressed against my heart.
All of my flesh was a thick foliage
Where the wild dove was moaning.

VII

Yes, it is true: I am afraid.
My hands can't grasp the columns of the earth,
My heart can't hold familiar faces,
My house turns and the buzzing is too loud and a white-haired
    woman, a beautiful woman I once loved,
Whose face is now a moon hurled into silent waters
Is calling out my name. I hear my childhood name being uttered
    slowly, clearly:
"Are you there?"
            "Yes, I am here, oh pale relic of generous love."
            "You are not there, you are not there, your milk
            weakens as it mixes into drops of night,
            your sword throws out flames and you tremble,
            a gust of wind sweeps away your soul,
            you can't resist possessing yourself."
Once again I hear my cradle rocking over the waves,
The solitary fisherman's song wets my temples,
The captive albatross shakes its wings,
And this soothes me a little.
Holding a brazier, I dance on the turbulent waters,

I dance among the ruins of the city
Among terrifying prophecies
While the shadows whisper in my ear
And put out the day of fire .

X

Is the invisible just another side of what is visible? The dead man,
    is he the half-closed side of himself?
Is there a separating wall, or just a changeable lamp
      which takes turns
             in giving us light?
And the dance unites us in a common presence
And my abstinence is satiety for my neighbor
And my crying is his laughter
And my heart is his grain bursting
And if by chance I give in, I will be nothing
But cane for the final scream to echo,
Even as I go on living.

XI

Hold back the dead man we carry within ourselves like an unruly
    guest!
Kill the premature young killing us,
Prune time's invisible branch
Which bristles in me, spreading the white head of hair over the
    things that I touch with affection.
The one leading the dance of death is not death but me.
I am the son and the father of my death
And while I gaze at it fixedly I make my life,
I know that I will be afraid when the final moment comes.
Why not be afraid at every instant?
I am the edge of a world without memory
The flower of a remote extasy.

XII

When will we understand a way of dying without life being merely
    an eve that lives within?
We touch each other as if we did not belong to ourselves and space
    comes out of things in disarray and infernal arabesques come out
    of the eyes.
When will the pupils pass through the thicket of eyelids, final masters
    of our suppositions?
Perhaps we are a pact between those great shadows that once
    wished to be united by time in order to understand their own
    enigmas.
        Oh, shadows of other shadows!
Maybe they lean over the poor elf in order to see themselves,
        they wish to feel confirmed and feared,
        familiar and portrayed.
And if those congregated shadows were to withdraw like the waves
    of a stormy sea,
Would that be the end of man?

(1947)

VISION OF LIKENESS

I am here
Holding on to my bed
Stiffled by my own breathing

I swim
Among great Rigid Waves

Passionately stuck to Threads
My flesh
Swirling noisily
Hollowing out

Alone
So alone
Covered in human shadows

Boring into my own belly
The wave I clench against me

I smell of weeping
Of dissected flowers inside an old book

Touching
That which collapses through
That which is always the same

I am friendly with the Horse
Cheerful
There are Horse spasms

They shot at me
I fell on my knees by the edge of the
Sea

I remain higher
Impenetrable
Placed like an angel holding
A blaze

I make the Sun's shadow
With these shut eyelids
The Sun's skeleton
Charcoal

There I stand out
As fine
As the trembling needle
Of a panting compass

(I hear the rumor
Of leaves
A windy silence)

Medusas
Cross my body
My wife approaches
A million vibrations approach

My eyes print the irate arrow
That crosses emptiness
I do not sing I do not speak
I merely insist on a terrestrial moon

Here is my soul
Wrapped around a wandering star
My circle of birds
Cut by lightning

It is the perfection of my suffering
The moon weighs on me
I open drawers full of
Snakes

I do not see you
I do not hear you
I contain you
My heartbeats are your steps

My face is
Gnawed by s i g n s
I flaunt
Ocean swells

Divide me
In the depths of human beings
Lighten the weight of my solitude

May only the lip
Surround me

More than existence I desire being
For the pleasure of being possible

Let us be
Immensely
In the presentiment of what is
Unfinished
Broken stones that make up a figure

To go against ourselves
Would it relieve us of the stupor of being
Without hope
Other than the dispersal of ourselves?

I file down my teeth
The splinters in my crown my horns
Turn them into sharp points

My enemies ride
With stirrups made of ice

I kick with my heels
The b l i n k i n g waters
Mule trader
Untangling cloths that embalm
Swans

Athlete lifting the
Sea
The Sea
The boiling scab of an
Ancient
Abolished dream

I renounce my faith in what I am
In what I am not
I seek to prolong
My soul among visions

I search I search
The vibrant the prophetic
Plenitude of my body

I am surrounded by
Broken chairs   food leftovers
Nasal men who make
The oil boil

I swear that
My wounded conduct is the consequence
Of someone else's horror

My superstition
Is the sleepwalker's confidence

I sing
I am lined with magnets
I cross forgetting

With a painful vertigo with a
Stupid hat
I start nailing down two mouths

Suddenly
Everything is a sucking of bees
We die from bees

Oh
My wife
My beautiful long-eared one
My sorceress
My snowed loneliness

Reach me
Little star bones
Animals
That think sadly

A trembling nest
A sword of light like a sacred order
For my somber magnitude
To burst in s t r e n g t h

Come
Exorcise my eyes shattered
In dream
My bonfires of pale
Suns

Your fingernails
Poke
At roots of intertwined life

Like a blind man
Hitting the flowers with a cane
I drag myself without my likeness

Nascent
Ever more ephemeral
As though my life were a mere
Delay

Today I integrate myself to the Tiger
I need
A tree of Latin
Personifies me

Flight chairs   the chairs
Bleat

Through levitation
I raise a purely tactile being

I hear a scream
A song of stone
Half-opening the posthumous night

A word
Like the fusion of "blind echoes"
I must now
Sacrifice my limits

Where am I?
In what secret part of myself
Do I extend myself into non-being
And remain what I am?

The dilation
of the f o r e h e a d begins

These hands these
Feet
Can no longer be reached

These eyes
Begin to sink

These ears
Are no longer outside

Outside
Just the sea   the sea
With its dreadful drunkenness

Everything turns to silence
As if the   T i g e r ' s   pulse
Came to a halt

I am threatened by
The blood dancing on the
Mirror

I am the Zenithal little man
The Man
With the Whistling Head of Hair

Holding on
To floods of blood

("Therefore I have cried
Concerning this. Their
Strength is to sit still"
Isaiah XXX 7)

Nothing of what I am
Must be omitted from me
Not the beast
Rubbing itself with the S u n

Not the angel
So pale
As though squeezed by atrocious
Hands

I am
The vertigo
Of my m o r t a l   s t a t e s

Who am I
I who so closely resemble what I should be?

As though a
Ghost
Were moving these joints

I stare at the ceiling
It seems to be propped up by
Lightning

I flee
I hang myself from a sky made of stone

They spread out
my bones

I have a Starfish
Encrusted
In my wooden leg

I am alone
Lone stump of a candle absorbed
Alone
At the center of space

Alone
Near the final will
At the end of each will

The Flux
Of unheard-of substances

The pulsation of Nothingness
Grows

My sweat
Runs down the walls

My wife advances groping her way
Her Hair of Salt
Sheared

An agonizing sky swirls
Around her
Her lips suck
At a sky of bloody sponges

She undresses
She takes off her snake skins

One by one
She hangs them from the air until they fill
The night

She gleams in her   n a k e d n e s s
Stretched by the moon

I place the Emerald
On her Navel

Shake oh thunderous statue
At the edge of nothingness

Woman
Your eyes are Fire
Rubbing against death

I drown you in your flesh
I wring you
Until the Poppy liquor begins to run

A deep Dream
Masks us

Dream that takes my Being
Back to my Birth

I begin to torment
Birth
I move my germinating lips

I move my eyes   like the sparks
Of another Perpetual Eye

Weeping is flowing out of your breasts
You suckle
A greening shadow

Such is
The slowness of our deathbed
The natal bed I cling to

Alas

I just want to welcome the Forms
Rider of swans
To lie down on a layered Sea
Flee the outcome

I want to stick the hummingbirds to my body
As though everything were foreign to me
Save the impossible

Taster of the clot

I drag myself
Smoking pieces of darkness

Inside me
I touch the knife-edge
Of a now finished star

I touch myself lasciviously
I love myself   with hate

Humberto Díaz-Casanueva   *281*

On this night
With these anointed fingers
I stretch   the eyes of the dead

Holes
In the luminous bread
Baked in my soul

(1970)

BIOGRAPHICAL NOTES

The list of works after each author's biography is not meant as a complete bibliography but merely as a guideline for the reader. Unless otherwise indicated, all listed titles are poetry collections.

Eduardo Anguita. Chile 1914-1992. Tireless promoter of avant-garde influences in Chilean literature, most specially of the *creacionista* philosophy as proposed by Vicente Huidobro whose rightful heir Anguita considered himself to be. In 1935 he co-edited with Volodia Teitelboim the landmark anthology*Antología de poesía chilena nueva*. He claimed that there existed a literary movement called "David" which no one knew about and of which he was the leader. Anguita was awarded Chile's "Premio Nacional de Literatura." He died tragically of burns sustained after accidentally tripping over a space heater in his home.

Inseguridad del hombre (1950), *Anguita* (1951), *El poliedro y el mar* (1962), *Venus en el pudridero* (1967), *Poesía entera* (1970), *Antología poética* (1973), *Nueva antología de poesía castellana: España, Hispanoamérica, Chile* (editor, 1981), *El poliedro y el mar: seguido de La visita* (1984), *La belleza de pensar* (essays, 1988), *Definición y pérdida de la persona* (1988).

Braulio Arenas. Chile 1913-1988. Principal animator with Enrique Gómez-Correa of *Mandrágora*, the Chilean Surrealist group whose many activities included the publication of a magazine by the same name (1937-1941) and an international Surrealist exhibition held at Galería Dédalo in 1948 in Santiago de Chile. Edited the magazine *Leitmotiv* (1941) and *Actas surrealistas* (1974), an anthology of surrealist texts. Arenas translated seminal works of French literature into Spanish, including Rimbaud's *Une saison en enfer* and *Poésies* by Isidore Ducasse. He was awarded Chile's "Premio Nacional de Literatura."

El mundo y su doble (1940), *La mujer mnemotécnica* (1941), *Luz adjunta* (1950), *En el océano de nadie* (1952), *La gran vida* (1952), *La casa fantasma* (1952), *Poemas* (1960), *Pequeña meditación al atardecer en un cementerio junto al mar* (1966), *Adiós a la familia* (fiction 1966), *La endemoniada de Santiago* (fiction 1969), *El castillo de Perth* (fiction 1969), *En el mejor de los mundos* (1970), *Berenice: la idea fija* (fiction 1975), *Una mansión absolutamente espejo deambula insomne por una mansión absolutamente imagen* (1978).

José María Arguedas. Peru 1911-1969. Born in Andahuaylas, in the sierras of southern Peru, Arguedas spent most of his childhood among Quechua speaking Indians, an experience that marked him deeply and which defines all of his literary and anthropological work. His enormous contribution to the understanding of Peruvian folklore can be gleaned through his translations and compilations: *Mitos, leyendas y cuentos peruanos* (1947), *Canciones y cuentos del pueblo quechua* (1949) and *Cuentos magicorrealistas y canciones de fiestas tradicionales en el valle de Mantaro* (1953).

Arguedas is internationally known for his novels and shorts stories which have been widely translated: *Agua* (1933), *Yawar Fiesta* (1941), *Diamantes y pedernales* (1954), *Los ríos profundos* (1958), *El Sexto* (1961), *Todas las sangres* (1964), *Amor mundo y todos los cuentos de José María Arguedas* (1967), *El zorro de arriba y el zorro de abajo* (1971). His poetry, originally written in Quechua and translated by him into Spanish, is collected in *Katatay* (1984). He committed suicide on December 2, 1969.

Jorge Cáceres. Chile 1923-1949. Joined the group "Mandrágora" at a very young age and collaborated in its publications and exhibitions with poetry and collages. His poems appear in international Surrealist publications of the 1940's such as *VVV* and *Tropiques*. Jorge Cáceres was principal dancer of *Ballet Joos* in Santiago de Chile. A few hours after a performance in 1949, Cáceres suffered a fatal heart attack.

René o la mecánica celeste (1941), *Pasada libre* (1941), *Por el camino de la gran pirámide polar* (1942), *Monumento a los pájaros* (1942), *Textos inéditos* (1979).

César Dávila Andrade. Ecuador 1918-1967. Began writing poems of pastoral inspiration about his native country but soon moved on to larger, even epic poetry that expressed the power of the historical past and the desolation of the present. Dávila Andrade, who was also a short story writer, has had a profound influence on the literature of Ecuador.

He led a precarious existence most of his life and committed suicide while living in Caracas, Venezuela in 1967.

Espacio, me has vencido (1946), *Consagración de los instantes* (1950), *Catedral salvaje* (1952), *Abandonados en la tierra* (fiction 1952), *Boletín y elegía de las mitas* (1954), *13 relatos* (fiction 1955), *En un lugar no identificado* (1960), *Conexiones con la tierra* (1964), *La corteza embrujada* (1966), *Cabeza de gallo* (fiction 1966), *Materia real* (1970), *Obras completas* (1984).

Humberto Díaz-Casanueva. Chile 1907-1992. The years of his youth spent at the University of Jena in Germany studying the philosophy of Nietzsche and Heidegger left a profound mark on his poetry and world view. His own definition of his poetic impulse as ''magical and pre-metaphysical intuition'' shows his affinity with German Romanticism and the admitted influence of Surrealism. Díaz-Casanueva's successful career as a diplomat culminated with his term as Chile's ambassador to the United Nations (1970-1973). He was awarded Chile's ''Premio Nacional de Literatura.''

El aventurero de Saba (1926), *Vigilia por dentro* (1931), *El blasfemo coronado* (1942), *Réquiem* (1945), *La estatua de sal* (1947), *La hija vertiginosa* (1954), *Los penitenciales* (1960), *El sol ciego* (1966), *Sol de lenguas* (1970), *Antología poética* (1970), *El hierro y el hilo* (1980), *Conjuro* (1980), *Los veredictos* (1981), *La Aparición* (1984), *El pájaro Dunga* (1985), *El niño de Robben Island* (1985), *Vox Tatuada* (1985), *Antología poética* (1986), *Obra poética* (1988).

Enrique Gómez-Correa. Chile 1915-1995. One of the most distinguished representatives of Latin American Surrealism, Gómez-Correa founded ''Mandrágora'' with Braulio Arenas (1937), the Surrealist group whose activities (including the magazine of the same name and its successor *Leitmotiv*) would revolutionize Chilean poetry. His essay *Sociología de la locura* (1942), which served as his as doctoral dissertation while at law school, provided the theoretical backbone for poets and artists close to Surrealism.

Las hijas de la memoria (1940), *Cataclismo en los ojos* (1942), *Mandrágora Siglo XX* (1945), *La noche al desnudo* (1945), *El espectro de René Magritte* (1948), *Lo desconocido liberado. Las tres y media etapas del vacío* (1952), *Mandrágora rey de gitanos* (drama 1954),

La idea de Dios y las vocales (1954), *Reencuentro y pérdida de la Mandrágora* (1955), *La violencia* (1955), *El calor animal* (1973), *Zonas eróticas* (1973), *Madre tiniebla* (1973), *Poesía explosiva 1953-1973* (1973), *Mother Darkness* (1975), *A Mayo/To Mayo* (1980), *La pareja real* (1985), *Frágil memoria* (1988), *El nombre de pila o el anillo de Mandrágora* (1989), *Las cosas al parecer perdidas* (1990).

Enrique Molina. Argentina 1910. Closely associated with Argentine Surrealism, co-founded with Aldo Pellegrini the magazine *A partir de 0* (1952). Molina, like few others, embodies the surrender of the self to the poetic spirit. He has given free reign to his desire to wander by sailing with the merchant marine for several years and has always allowed chance rather than his will to determine the course of his life. The end result is a body of work charged with hallucinatory and erotic power. Molina's incursion into fiction writing resulted in the lyrical and highly acclaimed historical novel *Una sombra donde sueña Camila O'Gorman* (1974). He was awared Argentina's "Premio Nacional de Literatura."

Las cosas y el delirio (1941), *Pasiones terrestres* (1946), *Costumbres errantes o la redondez de la tierra* (1951), *Amantes antípodas* (1961), *Fuego libre* (1962), *Las bellas furias* (1966), *Hotel pájaro* (1966), *Monzón napalm* (1968), *Amantes antípodas y otros poemas* (1974), *Obra poética* (1978), *Los últimos soles* (1980), *Páginas seleccionadas por el autor* (1983), *Obra completa* (1984), *El ala de la gaviota* (1989).

César Moro. Peru 1906-1956. Pseudonym of Alfredo Quíspez Asín. Unable to conform to the restrictive Peruvian society of his time, Moro lived most of his life in France (1925-1934) and Mexico (1939-1948). Intransigent, rebellious, Moro conceived of poetry as a means of subverting reality through the exploration of the unconscious and sexual desire. He co-founded with Emilio Adolfo Westphalen the magazine *El uso de la palabra* (1938). Also a visual artist, Moro co-organized with André Breton the International Surrealist Exhibition of Mexico. One half of his work is written in French. Moro's work survives thanks to the dedication of the French writer André Coyné.

Le Château de grisou (1943), *Lettre d'amour* (1944), *Trafalgar Square* (1954), *Amour à mort* (1957), *La tortuga ecuestre y otros poemas:*

1924-1949 (1958), *Los anteojos de azufre* (1958), *Love Till Death* (1973), *Versiones del surrealismo* (essays 1974), *Derniers poèmes. Ultimos poemas (1953-1955)* (1976), *La tortuga ecuestre y otros textos* (1976), *The Scandalous Life of César Moro, In His Own Words* (1976), *Obra poética* (1980).

Alvaro Mutis. Colombia 1923. Mutis' internationally acclaimed novels owe much in style to his literary formation as a poet. Associated with the group around the magazine *Mito* in Colombia, Mutis introduces us to the fictional character and protagonist of his novels *Maqroll* in an early book of poems, *Los elementos del desastre* (1953). Much like his fiction, Mutis' poetry is marked by nostalgia for the past and an almost existential resignation to the present. Both his poetry and fiction have been translated into the major European languages. Mutis has been awarded numerous literary prizes including the *Prix Médicis* (France) and the "Premio Nacional de Literatura" (Colombia).

Poetry collections: *La balanza* (1948), *Los elementos del desastre (1953), Reseña de los hospitales de ultramar* (1959), *Los trabajos perdidos* (1961), *Summa de Maqroll el Gaviero* (1973), *Caravansary* (1982), *Los emisarios* (1984), *Crónica y alabanza del reino* (1985), *Un homenaje y siete nocturnos* (1987), *Summa de Maqroll el Gaviero 1948-1988* (1990), *Les Eléments du désastre* (1993).

Fiction: *Diario de Lecumberri* (1960), *La mansión de Araucaíma* (1973), *La nieve del Almirante* (1986), *Ilona llega con la lluvia* (1988), *Un bel morir* (1989), *La última escala del "Tramp Steamer"* (1990), *Amirbar* (1990), *Abdul Bashur, soñador de navíos* (1991), *Empresas y tribulaciones de Maqroll el Gaviero* (1993).

Olga Orozco. Argentina 1920. Through a remarkably effective use of free association Orozco builds a personal imaginary world in which poetry is used as a tool to create visual and sensorial effects. Lyricism permeates all of Orozco's work including the narrations published under the title *La oscuridad es otro sol* (1967).

Desde lejos (1946), *Las muertes* (1951), *Los juegos peligrosos* (1962), *La oscuridad es otro sol* (1967), *Museo salvaje* (1974), *Veintinueve poemas* (1975), *Cantos a Berenice* (1977), *Mutaciones de la realidad* (1979), *Obra poética* (1979), *Antología* (1982), *La noche a la deriva*

(1983), *Obras de Olga Orozco seleccionadas por la autora* (1984), *En el revés del cielo* (1987), *Mutaciones de la realidad* (1992).

Aldo Pellegrini. Argentina 1903-1973. Poet and essayist, Aldo Pellegrini became the driving force behind Argentine Surrealism through magazines such as *Que* (1928-1930) and *A partir de 0* (1952-1956) and through his extensive writings on the visual arts. He edited and translated *Antología de la poesía surrealista* (1961), still considered the most representative anthology of French Surrealist poetry, as well as the notable *Antología de la poesía viva latinoamericana* (1966). Pellegrini is also known for his outstanding translations of Lautréamont's *Oeuvres* and Breton's *Manifestes du surréalisme*, among others.

El muro secreto (1949), *La valija de fuego* (1952), *Construcción de la destrucción* (1954), *Teatro de la inestable realidad* (1964), *Para contribuir a la confusión general* (essays 1965), *Distribución del silencio* (1966), *Confrontación del vacío* (1967), *Escrito para nadie* (1989).

Gonzalo Rojas. Chile 1917. Even though he was briefly associated with the Surrealist group "Mandrágora" and though he has made good use of the possibilities of renewal offered by the avant-garde, Rojas' work owes much to traditional Spanish poetry. Rojas puts these tensions to work as he expresses both metaphysical and social concerns. Rojas organized important international authors' festivals while at the University of Concepción (Chile), yet he has always maintained his independence from literary schools and styles. He was awarded Chile's "Premio Nacional de Literatura."

La miseria del hombre (1948), *Contra la muerte* (1964), *Oscuro* (1977), *Trastierro* (1979), *Del relámpago* (1981), *50 poemas* (1982), *Críptico y otros poemas* (1984), *El alumbramiento* (1986), *Esquizotexto y otros poemas* (1988), *Materia de testamento* (1988), *Desocupado lector* (1990), *La miseria del hombre* (1993).

Pablo de Rokha. Chile (1894-1968). Pseudonym of Carlos Díaz-Loyola. His work contributes a harsh, ultimately subversive element to the avant-garde style as adopted in its purified European form by de Rokha's contemporary, Vicente Huidobro. His sometimes excessive world vision is born of his peripatetic childhood spent in various places in Chile. During the 1930's he opts for political compromise and joins the Communist party which marginalizes him in 1940 as a result of his breakup with Pablo Neruda. He committed suicide in 1968.

El folletín del Diablo (1922), *Los gemidos* (1922), *Cosmogonía* (1925), *U* (1926), *Satanás* (1927), *Ecuación* (1929), *Suramérica* (1927), *Escritura de Raimundo Contreras* (1929), *El canto de hoy* (1932), *Canto de trinchera* (1933), *Jesucristo* (1933), *Los 13* (1935), *Moisés* (1937), *Gran temperatura* (1937), *Morfología del espanto* (1942), *Los poemas continentales* (1945), *Carta magna del continente* (1949), *Fuego negro* (1953), *Arte grande o ejercicio del realismo* (1953), *Antología 1916-1953* (1953), *Idioma del mundo* (1958), *Genio del pueblo* (1960), *Estilo de masas* (1965), *Mis mejores poemas* (1969).

Rosamel del Valle. Chile 1901-1965. Pseudonym of Moisés Gutiérrez. He was totally self-directed in his acquisition of literature, including the classics and modern French and American literature. Although del Valle participated actively in the literary life of the 1920's and 30's in Chile and translated several French surrealist works (including Breton's *Fata Morgana*), it is difficult to ascribe his work to any one literary school. He launched two literary magazines, *Ariel* (1925) and *Panorama* (1926), and worked as a reporter for the daily *La Nación*. In 1946 he was hired by the United Nations and settled in New York, a city which suited his temperament perfectly and where he wrote some of his most inspired poetry. After retiring from the UN in 1962, he returned to Chile in 1963.

Mirador (1926), *País blanco y negro* (1929), *Poesía* (1939), *Orfeo* (1944), *Las llaves invisibles* (1946), *El joven olvido* (1949), *Fuegos y ceremonias* (1952), *La visión comunicable* (1956), *La violencia creadora* (essay 1959), *El corazón escrito* (1960), *El sol es un pájaro cautivo en el reloj* (1963), *Adiós enigma tornasol* (1967), *Eva y la fuga* (1970), *Antología* (1976), *Elina aroma terrestre* (1983), *The Apostles' Bar and Other Poems* (1990), *Eva the Fugitive* (1990).

Ludwig Zeller. Chile 1927. Zeller's childhood spent in the Atacama desert of northern Chile is the source of much of his imagery. His early poetry is influenced by his readings and translations of the German Romantics. Using the image as chief poetic device, Zeller constructs a world beyond the rational, where dream and wakefulness cease to be considered as separate states. Also a visual artist specializing in collage, he founded with Susana Wald "Casa de la luna" (1967-69), a gallery and meeting place as well as a publishing house and magazine. In 1971 Zeller emigrated to Canada where a considerable part of his poetry has appeared in English translation. Zeller has published much of his work in luxury editions, in exhibition catalogues, and in a video produced for the XLIII Venice Biennal.

Exodo y otras soledades (1957), *Del manantial: Poemas 1957-1961* (1961), *Las reglas del juego* (1968), *Los placeres de Edipo* (1968), *Mujer en sueño, Woman in Dream* (1975), *Cuando el animal de fondo sube la cabeza estalla* (1976), *Alphacollage* (collages, 1979), *In the Country of the Antipodes 1964-1979* (1979), *50 Collages* (collages, 1980), *Eugenio Granell o la invención del dado* (1981), *Un camello perfumado jamás baila tango* (aphorisms 1985), *The Marble Head and Other Poems* (1986), *Ludwig Zeller: A Celebration* (1987), *Salvar la poesía quemar las naves 1954-1987* (1988), *The Ghost's Tattoos* (1989), *To Saw the Beloved to Pieces Only When Necessary* (1990), *Zeller Free Dream* (1991), *Tatuajes del fantasma* (1993), *Aserrar a la amada cuando es necesario* (1994), *Río Loa Estación de los sueños* (fiction 1994).